NAMU
QUEST FOR THE KILLER WHALE

NAMU

QUEST FOR THE KILLER WHALE

Ted Griffin

Illustrations
Val Paul Taylor

Gryphon West Publishers

Cover photograph   Flip Schulke, Black Star
                    ©National Geographic Society

Published by   Gryphon West Publishers
                    801 E. Harrison Street, No. 105
                    Seattle, Washington 98102

ISBN: 0-943482-00-3

1 2 3 4 5 6 7 8 9 10
First Edition   October 1, 1982   Hardcover

Library of Congress Cataloging in Publication Data

Griffin, Ted, 1935—
    Namu, quest for the killer whale.

    Includes index.
    1. Namu (Whale)   2. Griffin, Ted, 1935—
3. Killer whale.   4. Killer whale—Biography.
5. Animal trainers—United States—Biography.   I. Taylor,
Val Paul.   II. Title.
QL795.W5G74   1982   599.5′3   82–81787
ISBN 0–943482–00–3   AACR2

in the name of the best within us

Ayn Rand, *Atlas Shrugged*

TABLE OF CONTENTS

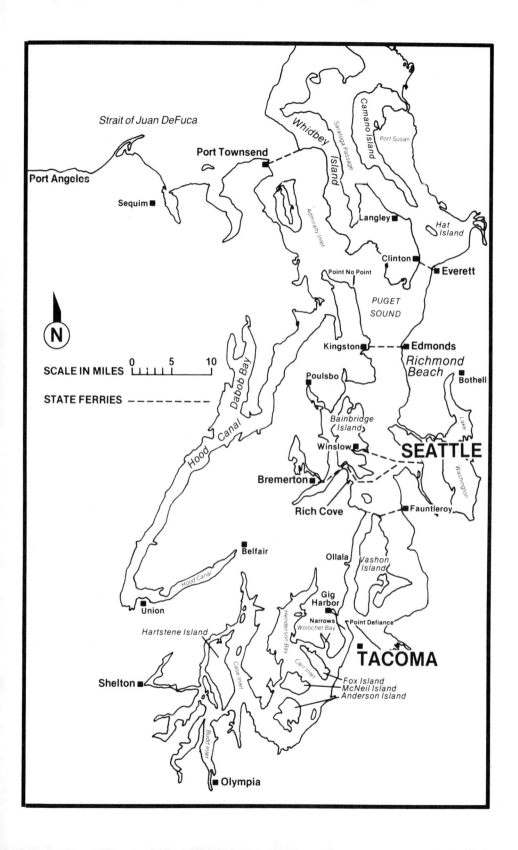

FOREWORD

Ted Griffin was, in his youth, the "Tom Sawyer" of Puget Sound. His fascination with wildlife, his inquisitive mind, his whimsical sense of humor, his kinship with other living creatures, including humans, and his insatiable appetite for adventure win him that title.

I first met Ted in 1962 when he needed veterinary medical advice in the care of a fur seal, a harbor seal, and an Atlantic bottlenose dolphin named Ivan. I introduced him to two colleagues of mine who later became whale veterinarians for him, and I followed his progress of whale catcher, trainer, and keeper with both professional interest and personal pleasure.

I soon learned not to be astonished at Ted's ingenuity, stamina, and persistence, not to mention his many talents and skills. Ted's main fault, perhaps, was his impatience which, not infrequently, got him in hot water.

Some prominent citizens and scientists indulged in the erroneously negative conclusion that Ted Griffin was motivated only by the desire to hear the cash register cling. How could they be so blind? There are literally hundreds of easier ways to make a living or a fortune.

Ted's fortune never materialized; furthermore, he gave up the comforts of home, family, and material benefits for the next ten years to search for another, less controversial, way of life, but that is another incredible story in itself.

If anyone should ask "what did Ted Griffin accomplish?", I can answer with authority that by the single act of going into the water with Namu, Ted Griffin contributed more to the conservation and appreciation of killer whales by societies of the world than all the biologists and conservationists put together, from the dawn of time to that moment.

But there is much more to be told, and I would be proud if Ted were to say that my encouragement and appreciation for what he did played a part in his decision to tell it.

What you are about to read is the greatest animal story ever written. It surpasses all fictional animal stories; yet every exciting word is true.

Now don your imaginary wet suits and go with Ted Griffin to the bottom of the sea to meet Namu, and commune with this magnificent leviathan until you are overtaken by the uncanny feeling that you yourself are a killer whale.

Mark C. Keyes, D.V.M.

Dr. Keyes has been a marine mammal research veterinarian for twenty years in the federal government's Fish and Wildlife Service and National Marine Fisheries Service. He has authored or coauthored over thirty scientific publications on marine mammals. He is a founding member and former president of the International Association for Aquatic Animal Medicine, and a former two term president of the Seattle Zoological Society. He is presently Consulting Veterinarian to the Seattle Aquarium and a member of the Board of Directors of the Seattle Aquarium Society.

PREFACE

My association with Namu, the memories of that lovable leviathan, will haunt me until the end of my life. All the while I was testing, teasing, and exploring the killer whale's nature, he was weaving a masterful web; ultimately holding me hostage for his own designs. After Namu died I wanted to record our unique interaction, yet fourteen years later not much had been accomplished.

By chance I met Dr. Mark Keyes, a long-time friend whom I hadn't seen in years. We had both been drawn to see a baby sperm whale brought to Seattle in 1979 after stranding on the Oregon coast. Watching the youngster which was suddenly thrust into a strange environment, my subconscious took me back to the time when I had entered a whale's world. Mark suggested I try again to write about Namu, and what had set me on such an unusual quest, to befriend one of the most feared and deadly animals on earth.

I started working that same day, but more was needed than enthusiasm and a will. A good friend, Barbara O'Steen, agreed to organize my material and rewrite when needed. For three years she was editor, and the major source of support and encouragement. This book is possible because of her important contribution.

NAMU
QUEST FOR THE
KILLER WHALE

1
The Quest

A huge black fin rose slowly out of the sea. Kneeling in a little rowboat, unable to move or breathe, I waited and watched. The most wondrous creature I had ever seen was just a few feet away. I was face to face with a killer whale! His saber-like dorsal fin towered over me. The fearsome predator looked like an executioner. Little wonder the sight of these enormous black and white creatures had caused so much terror.

Whoosh! I recoiled at the sound of the whale's breathing. My fingers locked on the gunnel. The whale, largest in the pod, held motionless, staring at me. Had I come too close to his family? The orca's incredible killing ability was legendary. I respected that aspect of his nature, but somehow did not feel he would injure me. What if all those stories about being dangerous to man were false? What if the killer whales were actually as friendly as dolphins? Though frightened, I felt a powerful urge to know this whale.

The bull submerged. I peeked over the rail. Directly under the little boat, he rolled onto his side. He was huge, four times the length of my fragile six-foot skiff. His snow-white underbelly and chin contrasted sharply with his brown inquisitive eye. Etched in a field of black behind his dorsal fin was an elegant design of white markings, reminding me of a nobleman's coat of arms.

His unblinking eye was looking directly at me. I felt a rush of excitement. I closed my eyes and envisioned us swimming together. I imagined reaching out; he allowed me to touch him. My hands traveled along his body. I murmured, "I want to be friends, to learn your secrets. How can I get through the barrier of our vastly different worlds?"

I could almost hear him answer, *Barriers? There are none, save those misconceptions which you carry, those limitations YOU impose.*

I struggled to retain my connection with the whale, but the spell broke. One swift stroke of his powerful tail and he vanished. Our time together was only a few seconds, yet it was rich with possibility. I felt impelled to discover the door to his world and the key to unlocking it.

This encounter in 1961 when I was twenty six was my first close contact with a killer whale, *Orcinus orca*, orca for short; and marked the beginning of the quest which brought me into contact with a magnificent animal four years later. My story really begins many years before, when I was a boy growing up in the Pacific Northwest. Along the west coast of the United States and Canada, killer whales are local inhabitants, especially in the Puget Sound area of Washington State.

I was four when my parents divorced. The next few years my younger brother Jim and I lived part-time with our mother in Everett, Washington, a mill town on Puget Sound just north of Seattle. "You can't take those beach crabs to bed with you, Ted," Mom would protest, then tuck me in and read a chapter from the *Count of Monte Cristo*. She taught me to play poker, "Learning the rules is easy; it's knowing when to bet, how to keep a straight face, and the art of bluffing that makes you a winner." If Jim and I wanted to go to a movie, Mom left us near a vacant lot to hunt the price of admission in refundable bottles.

After Mom remarried, becoming Nancy Spaeth, the four of us spent many wonderful summers at a Whidby Island beach cabin, a few miles north of Seattle and a twenty-minute ferry ride from the mainland. Bill Spaeth was kind to Jim and me, patiently teaching us seamanship, the skills of fishing different tides for salmon and cod, and respect for the sea and all that dwelled there. I thought he knew just about everything.

"You'll need large hooks and lots of lead, boys," my stepfather said one day when I was ten. "We're after the big lunkers in Glendale hole."

"Big lunkers? How big are they? How deep is the hole? Let's go."

His blue eyes twinkled as he answered, "Well, Ted, you'll just have to find out for yourself. You and Jim should have an even chance with the fish, though. You're about the same size."

Jim and I ran ahead down the beach to watch several men drag their boat over a series of driftwood skids to a point above the high tide line. "Any action?" I asked.

One fellow held up a cutthroat trout for our inspection, "That's about it."

"We toss the wee ones back," my stepfather said; "let 'em grow a bit."

"Ahh, you laugh," he replied. "Well, there aren't going to be any fish caught around here for awhile!"

"Oh? And why is that?"

"Because them dadblame blackfish are in! They got the salmon so spooked they just quit biting." *Is a blackfish something like a shark?* I wondered.

"Look-a-there! What'd I tell you? There goes a blackfish now." Everybody looked toward the channel, but I saw nothing unusual. "Ahh those good-for-nothing pesky whales! It's uncanny how they always show up just when the salmon are running real good. It's like they, like someone tells them." *Whales?*, I thought to myself, *like the one that swallowed Jonah? and Pinocchio? Right here in front of the beach house?* I was bursting with questions.

A soft-spoken man wearing a green hat with tied-up earflaps told how he was chased to shore by several whales while fishing near Possession Point.

"Chased, huh?" exclaimed his companion. "One of those son-of-a-guns crashed right into my skiff. I thought I was a goner! Probably would have been too, if it had been a killer whale."

"What's a killer whale?" I asked, but they ignored me.

"I take no chances," said an elderly man with a cane. "Whenever they show up around my boat I just head for shore and wait until they're gone."

A burly fellow in a red plaid jacket added, "They're dangerous; they'll kill anything that gets in their way, including a man. I carry my 30-30 right in the boat, and shoot them every chance I get."

With a reassuring smile our stepfather put his arms around us, "Come on, boys; let's show them how to catch fish. Killer whales, blackfish, they don't bother me and I don't bother them. We have a gentleman's agreement."

The three of us picked favorite places at the end of the deteriorating Glendale dock, once a busy cargo ship and foot-passenger stop on the east side of Whidby Island. I clambered up onto a pile of lumber and with a great heave cast all the loosely piled fish line far out, then scanned the horizon. Earlier visions of landing a big lingcod were replaced with thoughts of whales. *Can they get us here?* I wondered, *on this high dock?* In the clear water a group of common pile perch swam in the sunlight, occasionally darting into the shadows. My stepfather said, "Those perch are feeding on wood worms and barnacles."

"How could anything eat those tough old barnacles?" I asked. He only smiled

Something surprised a school of fat little candle fish. Like frightened sheep they turned simultaneously, each instinctively following in the path of another.

One of the fishermen told us he had seen seals jump out of the water right onto the beach to escape a horde of hungry whales. I had seen spotted harbor seals swimming in the shallows near our cabin and thought, *Do whales eat them? Could a whale swallow a seal whole?* I took up the slack in my line and leaned over to look at the perch again. *Do blackfish whales eat perch?* Suddenly the stack of lumber shifted; I toppled and fell—down—down—down.

"Uhhh!" The shock of entering the frigid water took my breath away, but I thrashed and kicked to keep afloat. I tried to watch for sea monsters coming, but the salt water burned my eyes. *Will they eat me?* Then I imagined a friendly whale coming to my rescue.

A man tossed his cap and jumped in beside me, grabbing my shirt. I heard shouting. A small boat came alongside; I reached for the transom. After an eternity my feet touched bottom. Somehow I found the strength to walk ashore. My stepfather put his arms around me and began rubbing vigorously. When I broke into an embarrassed smile, he played his favorite role of a tease, "Well, Ted, you didn't get your ears clean. Best go back and scrub a little harder."

Nearly everyone expressed some personal fear as they talked about the accident. I didn't share their concern. Instead, that experience of hearing about whales and falling into their watery home at first frightened me, then whetted my appetite to learn more about them. It was as if the whale-talk and my plunge into the ocean had etched my subconscious, forging a psychic link with killer whales.

When we returned to the cabin Mom asked about my wet clothes.

"Ted heard some killer whales were around and got so excited he jumped in," my stepfather said with a wink. "Luckily a fellow launched a rowboat and fished him out just in time."

My mother responded, "Let's get you dry, and I'll tell you about the time I met some killer whales. Before you were born, George Clark and I were taking turns rowing a little boat around Hat Island. Suddenly we were surrounded by hundreds of whales. It gave us such a fright we each took an oar and rowed the whole two miles back to Clinton without stopping."

Several years later our father, Ed Griffin, took Jim and me on a summer vacation to one of the San Juan Islands, an hour's ferry ride from Anacortes, Washington. We stayed with friends on their small private island. Happy to be on my own and eager to explore, I set out at daybreak, my mind filled with thoughts from a book I had recently read, *Island Stallion* by Walter Farley. As if in answer to my thoughts, I saw a horse in the distance.

It took a while to quietly approach the horse on Charles Island. "Please don't run away." I held out a wad of limp, sweaty grass. His ears were straight up, twitching slightly, his nostrils dilating. I felt his hot breath on my hand. He nuzzled my fingers and ate the grass. Again and again I tried to pet him, but each time he held his head high, pulling back as I reached. I turned slowly and walked away, not looking back, and could hear his footsteps close behind. Each morning for the rest of the visit, I smuggled carrots and apples from the icebox and called on my new friend.

During frequent outings to the nearby islands in search of clams and crabs, I watched for a glimpse of a whale. Oliver, the grocer across the channel, had told me, "Yes, the blackfish often come by, especially during the summer, but there's no telling when, just when you least expect them."

Alone one clear day on a rocky bluff overlooking the Straits of Juan de Fuca, I saw the Olympic Mountains along Washington's coast. Turning west I could see all the way to

Victoria, British Columbia. On the horizon I momentarily caught sight of several black objects glistening in the early-morning sunlight. Plumes of white mist rose from the water. I heard whispering, a sound like waves softly washing onto the beach. Could they be fins? Of killer whales? My heart pounded. They were coming closer. The water was nearly calm except for the rippling gurgle of the running tide. Again I saw the plumes of mist, and about five seconds later heard a soft puff, puff, puff. I stood transfixed, breathing sounds reverberating through me. The whales rooted about in a nearby kelp bed, searching for something. When they surfaced with long strands of amber-colored bull-kelp draped across their fins, they reminded me of parading heroes draped with ticker tape. This was the closest I had ever been to whales. Though they revealed little of themselves, vanishing as mysteriously as they had appeared, I felt a strong rapport with them. Even before I could walk, the family's two English mastiffs had been my constant companions. I began thinking of the whales as friendly creatures, like horses and dogs, even though most people's attitudes differed sharply from mine. "Like sharks, they'll attack without provocation," they said, adding, "yeah, they're dumb, cold-blooded fish."

I was unwilling to change my view, that I could befriend any animal.

Some of the time Jim and I lived with our father on Gravelly Lake near Tacoma, Washington. He was a businessman, operating a home delivery fuel company. We talked a lot about business, economics, and politics. He always had an opinion, and could back it up with facts. He had a dry wit and frequently commented on the humorous side of world events. He liked to poke about the countryside looking in barns for antique automobiles to restore. On the fourth of July everyone looked forward to our big aerial fireworks display over the lake.

Dad loved sports. He taught all his children to swim and I spent much of my time underwater, watching the lake bass spawn, and netting a variety of fish that I maintained in a large goldfish pond. A neighbor boy often rode his horse in the lake. I wanted more than anything to have a pet like his and do the same.

"Ted is like a whale," Dad would say to his friends. "Stays in the water so much he may even turn into one."

When neighbors built a diving helmet out of an old water tank, I borrowed it. Using lead weights tied to my sneakers, I explored the lake bottom as long as anyone was willing to operate the bicycle pump which brought air to me through a rubber hose. I read a story about two Frenchmen, Émile Gagnan and Jacques Cousteau, who had invented an underwater breathing apparatus, basically a tank of compressed air and a regulator. I immediately sent for one. At long last I could remain underwater for an hour or more. The following year I purchased a rubber diving suit and plunged into the cold waters of Puget Sound.

Underwater became my second home. When the air supply was exhausted I resented having to surface. I wanted to stay all the time in that other world. A girl friend was once heard to complain, "How would YOU like to play second fiddle to an Aqua-Lung?"

Only the most miserable weather forced me to remain indoors. While building tunnels and laying track for my Lionel train, I listened to records of Tarzan, the ape-man who made friends with jungle animals. I read the *Wizard of Oz* many times, and dreamed of living in a city just as fantastic.

As my interest in tropical fish grew, the *Innes Book of Fishes* became my favorite. I constructed a number of large aquariums in my father's fuel-truck repair shop, where the garage foreman taught me welding and metal fabrication.

Years later those skills proved valuable for building aquarium tanks, and constructing a giant cage to transport a whale.

During my high school years I frequently drove to the Tacoma Municipal Aquarium in Point Defiance Park to visit the curator, Cecil Brosseau. He taught me a great deal about marine mammals, and about how to set up and care for sea life displays. He offered to exchange specimens from his adequate reserves when I began my Seattle aquarium. A tall, slender Frenchman who usually dressed in white denim coveralls, he was constantly on the move. His manner and dress belied the man's depth of knowledge about local marine life and the responsibilities he carried. When Cecil talked, I followed his footsteps closely, in order to hear above the continuous splash of water. His voice carried a reverence when he spoke of the biggest marine mammals, the whales.

"Do killer whales ever show up around here?" I asked.

"Oh, sure, one of the crew was fishing lingcod in the Narrows this morning and saw a pod swimming off the point."

"Do you think they're still around?"

"Not likely. They usually don't stay in one place very long. If they swam south through the Narrows, they might stay awhile. There are hundreds of square miles of bays and inlets down that way. Don't worry, they're sure to come again, though they don't post a schedule."

"But all those stories, Cecil, attacking boats, attacking men!"

"Probably just that, Ted, stories."

As a teenager I thought it strange for killer whales, *Orcinus orca*, to travel with blackfish, *Globicephala*, also called pilot whales. The orca were known to kill other whales. People around Puget Sound called most of the whales blackfish, but the ones with very slender dorsal fins, five to six feet tall, I knew to be killer whales. Most animals observed had short, triangular, broad-based fins, curved on the trailing edge. Often the two types were together. Later I learned that the local sightings were all of orca, the shorter fins belonging to the females and immature animals. Though pilot whales are similar in size to adolescent orca, they like warmer water and are very rarely seen in cold Puget Sound.

Yearning for the sea, I returned home after two unfruitful years at Colorado College and located a job in a fish hatchery, then a retail pet shop. Others said, "But it's only a hobby, Ted. You should become a doctor, or a businessman, or—." I couldn't relinquish the desire to rear tropical fish. Eventually I was operating three pet stores, a wholesale pet-supply business, and manufacturing aquariums.

When I met Joan Holloway I was twenty-four, a confirmed bachelor and already a workaholic, totally immersed in the pet shop business. Nearly two years later, in 1961, we were married. That summer we rented a cottage at Richmond Beach on Puget Sound. The lure of the sea was irrepressible. Nearly every day I found some pretext to be on the water. If the wind blew hard I plowed into the surf, swam out to catch a big wave, and had a wild ride all the way to shore.

Popping to the surface one day, I surprised a fisherman by yelling, "Any luck?"

"Oh! ah, hello there," he replied. Turning his outboard skiff toward me he continued, "Naw, it's been a slow day."

As I flipped a live fish into his boat bare-handed, I grinned, "Well, no need to go home skunked."

Looking at me in wide-eyed wonder he exclaimed, "Where the devil did you get that big cod?"

"I keep a boatload of them down here." And I really did, a sunken lifeboat that attracted the fish.

During the summer I explored my underwater sanctuary, sometimes allowing the current to carry me several miles up the coast. In shallow water, flounders hid in the sand with only their eyes showing. On deep dives I saw ratfish undulating their pectoral fins, looking like birds in flight. Orange sea pens anchored in the sand spread their plume-like filtering fans to capture plankton. Though having the appearance of flowers, sea pens are actually animals. I often found tiny octopus, blennie eels, and sailor-fish residing in bottle-glass houses which collected offshore from a public beach. These modern apartments were endlessly fascinating. When the tide turned, the sea brought me home.

On a bright, crisp, September day I caught sight of a pod of whales just offshore, making their way toward my house. As they surfaced individually, I could hear distinct differences in their breathing sounds. One released its breath with a short, quick snort; another slowly, deliberately punctuating its exhalation with a raucous, sputtering sound. Their leisurely "strolling" manner and constant noise reminded me of happy, excited people on a Sunday outing.

Several of the big mammals poked their heads in the patch of kelp which marked the location of my "tame" fish residing in the sunken life boat. I wondered how many they had eaten or chased away. The tide was low; the water depth where they swam not more than six to eight feet. I had believed whales were afraid of stranding and always remained in deep water.

Quickly I had carried the small boat across the sand and rowed out, directly in the path of the whales. That was the first time I had come face to face with a killer whale. The few seconds we stared at one another were to have a profound effect on my life.

2
Launching The Dream

Six months later a friend burst into my office. "I see a gleam in your eyes, Duncan," I said.

"Come on, let's go for lunch," he suggested. "I have something I want to show you."

Crossing Seattle's Alaskan Way, he detoured, driving onto a waterfront pier. Standing in an empty warehouse he extended his arm and excitedly exclaimed, "You know what I think you could do here? Build a public aquarium! If you get started right away you could make it in time for the World's Fair."

I was startled by the suggestion, yet realized his idea was a natural for me. I could hardly contain my enthusiasm as he talked. Overnight I worked out rough plans and within a few days negotiated a lease for a portion of the block-long warehouse.

I asked friends and employees to work with me on the construction crew. Soon we were off and running, but progress was painfully slow. A visitor appeared and said, "I understand you're looking for some help."

Together we toured the aquarium site. Though his questions were few, he sized up every detail. "Mr. Griffin," he said, "I can do the whole job for you."

"The whole job? You mean building the aquarium?"

"Yes. I know exactly what has to be done and how to do it. You assign me overall responsibility and I'll get your aquarium built in time for the tourist season."

I liked his air of almost-arrogant confidence. His eyes looked calm, though they carried a fire. I realized he had

12

stopped speaking and was staring at me. I felt he knew what he was talking about and answered, "OK, it's a deal." *What an interesting turn of events*, I thought; *now I would have to follow orders.* It would be difficult, but if I could keep my ego suppressed, and he could deliver, I would come out way ahead.

The carpenter knew what he was doing. He saved us time, purchased materials at better prices, and kept everybody working happily. This individual had that unique spark of life I search for in people. He earned my respect. When later I learned he was recently recovered from a tragic accident, I guessed that the aquarium job was likely his first in some time. Our exchange was very rewarding.

Hearing that Steinhart Aquarium had some used glass to sell, Joan and I flew to San Francisco. After purchasing thirty-five panes of one-and-a-quarter-inch plate glass, we visited my favorite haunt, "Marineland of the Pacific," west of Los Angeles. Their performing pilot whales were like high-spirited ponies. I immediately wanted one. When Joan saw a photograph of a female killer whale, I asked for the manager. He told us the orca had been captured the prior year in nearby Newport Harbor. When I learned the killer whale swam in the Marineland pool without difficulty, I was fired anew to find one. The sea mammal's long-standing maladies probably caused her to remain in the shallow harbor, and also unfortunately caused her death. She lived in captivity just a few hours.

Members of the Puget Sound "Mud Sharks" diving team were eager to collect specimens for the new aquarium. I appreciated their endurance and superior diving skills, honed by years of competitive diving. We would be working in the water for most of each day's outing. Our first major expedition was to the San Juan Islands.

When we arrived, my friend Gary said, "The reef we're looking for is just ahead." The flashing orange light on the depth sounder stopped at one hundred feet. He called out, "Drop the hook."

"We sure made good time from Seattle, a little over four hours," a diver said.

"Yeah, not bad for a barge."

"Come on, Ted, I'll show you where to find the caves."

Down ninety feet I struggled to keep pace with Gary. The abundant, orange and white metridium anemones gave the whole area a garden-like appearance. When the outline of the reef loomed before us, we floated head-down and peered into dark caves. Gary pointed into one shadowy hole. I poked my head in, and quickly retreated from the snapping jaws of a lunging wolf eel. Gary gestured, *Grab him!*.

I motioned, *After you, fellow.*

He prodded with the net handle, agitating the mottled-gray critter until the six-foot eel darted squarely at us. Gary reacted swiftly. He spun around and looped the net over the frightful eel's marbled head. The powerful critter wriggled free several times; we recaptured it again and again. Finally the prize, a writhing, miniature "sea serpent," was put into our wooden holding tank.

Divers swam back to the boat towing a splendid assortment of sea life. Many varieties were not easily found in Seattle's then-polluted waters. Like opening Christmas presents, I unpacked the "goody" bags while the others plunged back into the sea.

Whoosh—whoosh. I turned, startled. Two bull orca had surfaced, almost within my reach! The tips of their dorsal fins rose higher than my head; and I am just over six feet tall. I saw whales everywhere, hundreds. So many, couldn't I get just one?

The graceful sea mammals appeared at random, heading in different directions. After a quick breath, each orca spiraled in a fast dive. *Such frisky behavior,* I thought. *Horseplay? Chasing after food? Of course.* Millions of salmon were on their way to spawn in nearby rivers. What the fishermen claimed must be true; killer whales understood the annual fish migrations.

My diving companions! I frantically searched for "boiling" patches of water, the divers' telltale trail of air bubbles. They looked normal. I thought the divers would hide among underwater rocks once they saw the orca. Shortly the sea mammals moved up the coast.

"Did you see the whales?" I anxiously asked each returning diver.

"What whales?" "What whales?" they echoed.

"The killer whales," I shouted, "dozens, hundreds of them. They swam right through you!"

No one had been the least aware of the potentially deadly animals. Surely the orca had noticed the divers. "Settle down, Griffin," Gary said. "I've seen killer whales around divers many times before. They've never bothered us, though I wouldn't want to jump smack in front of one to test the theory."

I thought, *killer whales ignore skindivers!* How could they tell the difference between the sea mammals which they reportedly ate, and humans? I could have swum right up to one. I had missed my chance!

In June of 1962 I opened my "Seattle Marine Aquarium" on schedule at Pier 56 along Alaskan Way, just in time for the World's Fair. A whale-shaped sign hung over the door, representing my dream.

Relaxing by the pier rail late one evening, I watched little figures of moonlight dance from wave crest to wave crest in the wake of a departing freighter. When the ship's navigation lights had faded, the reflected circles of light stood idle, as though waiting for another prime mover to pass that way.

Locking the door I began the nightly rounds. Something was wrong. The seawater supply to the fish tanks had stopped. They would all die! The pump was running free, but no suction. I checked the impeller for an air lock and tightened the shaft packing; still no water. *The intake line must be plugged. I'll have to go below.* Rushing to put on my wet suit, I tore the jacket. No time to fix it. I would need a flashlight. Darn, the battery was dead.

Carrying flippers, I descended the iron rung ladder. In the near-darkness under the dock I groped for the seawater-intake pipe and followed it vertically hand over hand, taking care to maintain contact with my underwater guide. At a depth of forty feet the pipe turned out along the bottom. I felt chilled as the cold water circulated freely through the tear in my jacket. Sloping down ever deeper, moving in total darkness, I told myself, *There's nothing dangerous down here.* Yet an unexpected adversary loomed —my prolific imagination. Hearing no sound except the reassuring hiss of my Aqua-Lung, I held my breath for long intervals, subconsciously trying to perceive a danger which I could not see. SMACK! Something slammed into my head, then was gone. Instinctively I raised my arm and brushed at my forehead. Something alive was down there with me. I was sure of it. Later I learned it probably had been a large shark.

Gathering my courage, I inched ahead. At last I came to the flange joint where the foot valve was attached. I reached beyond, feeling for some bit of trash covering the intake's protective grille. Suddenly my arm was grabbed and held firm, by a mass of thick, suction-cupped tentacles. From its strength I judged the devilfish to be enormous. My struggling only made it grip tighter. I grimly remembered reading that a Canadian diver's encounter with a four-hundred-pound octopus had put the man in a hospital.

With fierce concentration I relaxed; the hold slackened. I jerked my arm, breaking free. Gone? Cautiously I reached ahead, toward the foot valve. I sensed him near again! *Sure could use that flashlight now.* In the darkness I discovered one of his thick arms was snagged in the suction line.

I drew my knife from its scabbard, and with several brisk, sawing hacks, cut through the tentacle, but the octopus wrapped his arms about my head. *HE'S CLIMB-ING ONTO MY BACK.* I nearly panicked trying to avoid his poisonous beak. With both arms stretched overhead, I took a grip on his torso. It was massive; I could reach only part-way around. Still holding the knife, a last resort, I pressed my fingers inside his gill openings and squeezed violently. *LET ME GO, you fabulous animal! I don't want to kill you.* The octopus' grip slackened a little . . . then a little more. When I no longer felt his encircling arms I released the hold. The seven-armed marauder bothered me no more.

In the excitement, I had been gulping the air supply; now I could not fill my lungs. Pulling the emergency-air-reserve lever restored normal breathing. The stub of the severed arm protruded from the grille of the seawater-intake pipe. By touch I located and carefully removed two brass screws, retaining them in my mouth. Loosening the third screw, I swung the screen to one side. With considerable effort I unsnarled the rope-like tentacle from inside the foot valve. When I tried to replace the screws my numb fingers couldn't feel them. *And my air supply!* Again I labored for each precious breath. *I should surface. No!*

Over-riding the instinctive urge to gulp air, I patterned my breathing, delaying each shallow breath. Sensation

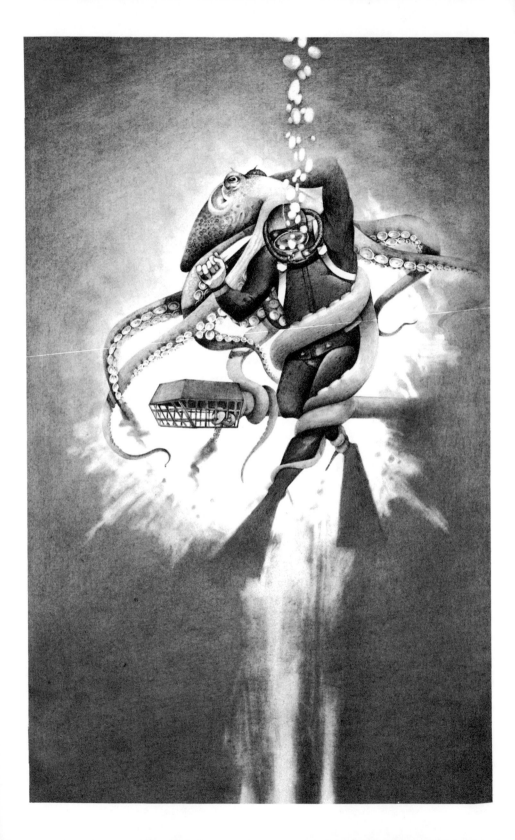

returned to my fingers by warming them inside the crotch of my wet suit. Quickly I inserted the screws.

As I drifted slowly upward, the reducing water pressure allowed release of additional air from the tank—the easier breathing a welcome reward. Perhaps I took too much of a chance, yet from many years of diving I had disciplined myself to work against the limit, recognizing and allowing for the effects of nitrogen narcosis. Knowing how long one can survive on an "empty" air tank is useful, like testing how long the car can operate when the fuel gauge indicates empty. In times ahead I would draw on these experiences.

During the ascent, occasional pinpoints of light passed by. Each glow emanated from a unique organism. In a way they represented very special individuals I had known: Duncan Bronson who envisioned the aquarium idea, Randy Mull the carpenter who helped me launch it, Gary Keffler who was ever ready with his expert diving skills, and many more. The increasing glare from the city penetrated the water, swallowing up the little sparks of life. Suddenly I felt alone.

Nearing the surface I instinctively raised my arm overhead to guard against bumping into some idle deadhead, rested a moment to get my bearings, then spotted the red warning lights along the piers, the lights that separated my two worlds.

3
Learning Process

My appetite for facts about *Orcinus orca* behavior was insatiable. I had to discover the true nature of the leviathan. Was a killer whale so directed by instinct that it could never be tamed? Perhaps it could be trained; food and fear usually worked, though I didn't know what it feared. But tamed? Coming to a human of its own free will, seeking interaction? The evidence pointed to just the reverse. The orca killed other mammals for food, and reportedly even for sport.

I searched for orca information in many books about whales, but they contained only sketchy accounts, mostly the same few known facts, hand-me-down stories, and legends. One book dealt exclusively with orca, but focused on the killer whale's nasty, unpredictable behavior. To my questions about interaction with humans, the answer seemed to be, "Don't! There's no future in it."

According to the studies, killer whales have been sighted in virtually every ocean of the world, though concentrate in the polar regions where they find an abundant food supply built upon the plankton chain. The orca's body is insulated from the frigid 32° water by a thick blubber layer; thus they can maintain a body temperature of 98° Fahrenheit.

Whales with teeth, *Odontocetid*, include the killer and sperm. The orca's forty-six to fifty conical teeth interlock with extremely close tolerances, averaging two inches in length above the gums. Sperm whale have similar but larger teeth present only in their very long, narrow, lower jaw; ideally suited for catching squid, a primary food source.

As whales go, the killer whale is not large. Nonetheless, when compared with humans, it is enormous. Mature bulls may grow to twenty-eight feet. The average length in Puget Sound is twenty-three to twenty-four feet. Thirty feet, and about eighteen thousand pounds, is record size. Adult females range up to twenty-two feet or so, weighing about ten thousand pounds. A newborn calf is six to eight feet long and weighs four hundred to six hundred pounds.

When early mariners observed a blowing whale, they often believed the visible plume was spouted water. Actually a small amount of water, trapped over the blowhole, is atomized into vapor as the whale expires each breath with great force. In cold climates the whales' warm, moist, expired air condenses into a towering plume, often visible for miles.

Scientists believe *Orcinus orca* evolved to their present form millions of years before *homo sapiens* started the long journey to dominance. In the sea the killer whale is dominant, ruling at the top of the food chain. They have achieved this position by using their well-developed brains, and have the apparent ability to select among alternatives and adapt to change. The orca brain weighs about six thousand grams. The human brain is roughly one quarter that size, though much larger in relation to body weight.

Fossil evidence shows that the sea mammals of today lived first in the sea; then left the water, adapted to life on land, and a few of those returned to the sea. Over millions of years, forearms changed into flippers of cartilage and muscle, yet the individual hand bones remain. Legs evolved back into tail flukes. A tough protective skin developed, supple yet strong. Its ability to stretch and bulge at high swimming speed substantially reduces drag.

The whale's skin also serves as a cooling system. When the animals migrate from the polar regions to warmer water, the blood flow is redirected, circulating close to the skin's surface. Excess heat is transferred into the water, cooling the body like a heat exchanger.

Whale species without teeth, *Mysticeti*, are thought to have evolved sometime later. With a mouth full of baleen plates, fibrous brushes serving as a filter, they extract tons of minute organisms from the sea. This ability to strain food gives them access to an almost limitless supply of microscopic plant and animal life called plankton, perhaps contributing to their evolving into the largest animal ever to inhabit the earth. The blue whale can exceed one hundred feet and one hundred fifty tons. It is *three times* larger than the largest land animal that ever lived, the ultrasaurus dinosaur, close cousin of the brachiosaurus dinosaur that weighed approximately fifty tons.

Each orca sighting in Puget Sound presented yet another opportunity to study killer whale behavior. I went out in my boat to be near them, watching for hours, trying to understand what they were all about, and imagining ways to capture one. People were learning about my efforts. A phone call from Portland, Oregon offered me a chance to participate in a killer-whale-capture trip with a veterinarian, a gunsmith, and an entrepreneur who offered to pay most of the expenses. He said he was going to display a killer whale in his Portland Sports Show.

"You are?!" I could hardly contain my excitement.

"I take it then, you would be agreeable to working with us."

I started to yell before I'd hung up the phone, "Pete! Is the boat ready to go?"

"Go? Go where?"

"After whales! I'm finally going out to capture one."

"Oh, really? You want me to skip lunch and get something ready to feed the new animal?"

"Come-on-Pete, you know what I mean."

"Yeah, sure, you want the boat ready to go yesterday. OK," he said smiling, "I'll do it." I liked having Pete working at the aquarium. He could fix almost anything, and his off-hand remarks offered me a rare mirror of myself.

I made plans for more employees, new signs, additional tickets, and lots of whale food. A week later my excitement reached fever pitch when a pod was sighted nearby, off Alki Point. I charged down the dock, "Oops!" and fell, tripping over my flying feet.

My friend on the Harbor Tour boat shouted from the bridge, "Hey, boy, where're you going in such a hurry?" I couldn't relax my vocal cords enough to answer as I leaped into "Pegasus," my twenty-three-foot, open runabout. Pegasus could fly me across the waves like the flying horse in Greek mythology.

In the Seattle harbor, near the mouth of the Duwamish River, I found the pod of ten to fifteen killer whales. Organized in a large circle, they pounded their tails, churning the water into a lather. Easing closer I saw a school of fish "boiling" at the surface. A salmon jumped clear of the water with a young whale in pursuit. The orca round-up of breakfast was a big success with distribution of profits immediate.

In less than two hours after my phone call, Bob O'Loughlin arrived from Portland with his two companions: Lee Estes the gun expert, alert, wiry, slightly built; and Dr. Mayberry, associated with the Portland Zoo. I picked them up in Pegasus and returned to the whales. Lee made ready his special rifle which fired syringe darts, while the veterinarian prepared the sedative mixture. Hopefully this would "tranquilize" a whale sufficiently to allow us to come alongside. When the animals surfaced, I revved the engine and chased after one. It was harder than I thought to get within range. Soon I realized they were definitely avoiding Pegasus; we must be spooking them.

"What we need is a helicopter," someone suggested.

I thought to myself, *wonder if Hertz rents them?* Then with sudden inspiration I headed for shore.

"Hello, this is Ted Griffin, director of the Seattle Marine Aquarium."

"Oh, yes, what can I do for you, Mr. Griffin?"

"I'm calling from the Coast Guard Light Station at Alki Point." I spoke in my most official-sounding voice, "We're doing some scientific studies with the killer whales in the harbor. Could your department provide us some assistance?"

The Seattle Police Department helicopter arrived shortly, landing on the lawn near the lighthouse. When I explained the mission the pilot looked excited. I removed the passenger door; Lee stepped in carrying his rifle, gingerly holding several of the syringe darts.

The helicopter climbed high above Puget Sound. Swooping like a hunting falcon, the chopper dropped out of the sky just as several whales rose to the surface. A red-tassled dart flew to its target.

"We got him!" I shouted, but the others reserved judgment. I was ready to maneuver Pegasus alongside the drugged whale the minute it slowed. An hour later I was worn out, still waiting in suspense.

To our great disappointment the muscle-relaxing drug had no apparent effect. Late in the day the drugged whale lingered at the surface. Cautiously I drew near. The crew was ready to put ropes around it. Just then a second whale appeared and pressed its chin to the back of the first animal. With one swipe, the aluminum cylinder was knocked away. The second whale had understood; it knew how to help! I was encouraged. They must have intelligence, and obviously cared for one another. My hope for future association with killer whales was reinforced.

When the day was lost Bob became philosophical, "Our first try, boys. When you take on something new like this, it's never easy." I felt sure we could solve the problem next time.

Several weeks later I received a phone call from Bob in Portland. He said, "I've asked Lee to work up something new in his gunshop. We'll be all set on this end in several days." I could hardly wait for our next outing, but no reasonable sightings were reported for a month.

When we next converged on the whales Lee unwrapped his customized, harpoon-firing rifle. I asked the veterinarian about the small-shafted harpoon, "Will it injure the animal?" He reassured me that it should do little harm to the whale, lodged in the thick blubber layer. A similar object was shot into the grey whales for tagging purposes. With the new approach I felt certain our big day had arrived.

After several frustrating hours in the helicopter, searching for an ideal-size whale, Lee harpooned one. It was easy keeping track of the whales by following the red buoys tied to the harpoon line. Lee joined us in Pegasus in order to fire a syringe dart of sedatives at the marked orca. To our amazement, every time the target animal rose to breathe, two other whales surfaced, one on each side, deliberately screening him. I found it impossible to get the marksman a clear shooting path as the three killer whales were inseparable. The trio traveled all day together and foiled our best efforts.

I decided the companion whales' protective action was a further display of intelligence, compassion, and the species' strong will for survival. They were smart enough to identify and avoid my boat. They hadn't rammed it as they once did a Marineland vessel in the San Juan Islands; those men had killed the whale to save the boat. I was confused over the stories of killer whale attacks. Maybe just certain orca were dangerous.

Toward evening the marker harpoon pulled free; we had no options left. The task of catching a whale was far more difficult than I had previously thought.

In the months that followed I experienced more disappointment in further capture attempts. When the Portland group was unable to come, I went without them. I modified a diver's spear gun and tried using it from a helicopter. More than once I reached a pod at dusk after a day of pursuit, only to have them vanish into the night. Expenses mounted. Finally I made a direct hit, but the spear bounced off the whale. Though a healthy whale had never been captured, I remained certain I would succeed. The female killer whale whose photograph I saw had been captured alive by Marineland, but it was very sick and probably had come to shore knowing it was going to die.

No closer to fulfilling the goal than a year ago, I realized my family and the aquarium were suffering. Maybe the quest was impossible, or some misconception concealed the solution.

In preparation for acquiring some dolphins, I eagerly approached the landlord. He thoughtfully assessed my proposal to lease additional space. The pier owner asked what calculations I had made for the water's weight, did I know the pier's loading capacity, and would the pool be large enough to house a whale? I had told him about my plans, and he wondered had I thought about using the adjacent waterway? Though his questions penetrated beyond the scope of my preparations, they stimulated my thinking. But his questioning tone seemed negative, as though he would refuse.

"All right, Ted," he said, holding back a smile, "I'll work with you on this one, but I want to see complete plans supported by an engineer's study."

I felt the urge to hug the conservative, impeccably dressed businessman, but contained myself. He was literally providing me a platform—a platform which would launch my career. He offered an initially low rent, to increase when I became successful. I and many others with limited capital and dreams to fulfill benefit from the actions of such individuals.

With the new lease in hand, and pool construction under way, I visited another marine exhibit that employed an animal trainer. He was on stage with his troupe of seals and sea lions, dressed in black boots and white britches. The ruddy, solidly built man was conducting a performance of his "Sea Circus" Show. His entertaining mix of humor, tricks, and serious routines gave the audience a clear understanding of the animals' natural inclinations and full capabilities.

When the show ended the sea mammals gathered affectionately about the showmaster, Homer Snow. I sensed their strong kinship with him. Feeling deeply moved, I asked him to work at the aquarium and to teach me about marine mammals.

A month after he started the new job, we received a shipment of two sea lions from California. I had been caring for them overnight and rushed out when Homer arrived in the morning. "They're going to starve to death, Homer! They won't eat the dead herring."

"Calm down, Ted. Just wait a minute." The veteran animal trainer returned with a food caddy strapped on a belt at his waist. "Watch this." Jiggling small squid in front of the new sea lion, Homer quickly aroused her appetite. "Come on, girl, that's it. Oh yes, you like that." Smacking his lips, mmmm-mmmm, he soon had her eating whatever fish were offered. "Gertrude" didn't bite, an unusual trait in a new animal, so she quickly made friends with all the staff.

The hip-swinging sea lion followed me like a puppy, begging for strokes, shining at my attentions. I was captivated by the sensitive animal, and took her home one night in the car. Frisky and curious, she climbed all over, then jumped into my lap, forcing me to the curb. My neighbors asked, "Who is that?"

"Gertrude? Why she's my new watch dog."

Though the sea lion learned her lessons and performed well, she annoyed Homer. One afternoon when she had climbed out of the big pool for the third time, he cautioned, "Very risky, Ted, one day she'll bite someone." She never did. I understood Homer's warning, but wanted others to meet the affable creature, to enjoy her company as I did, and thus allowed her the freedom of the aquarium. With a vigorous hug, youngsters often grasped the wet animal about the shoulders. Though separated by twenty years, I shared with children their unreserved joy, and an eagerness to explore whatever piqued our curiosity.

The second sea lion to arrive with Gertrude was a male we named Gus. His contrary personality made him rather unpopular, but he did respond to training. One evening when Homer was about to leave, he warned, "Keep a watch on Gus. He's off his feed." The sea lion's fur looked messy, his head hung down. Over the next few days I tried vitamins, antibiotics and forced feeding. Our veterinarian diagnosed parasites and other problems, not life-threatening in the wild, but the trauma of recent capture had destroyed Gus' balance of health. Others didn't think he was worth the time, but I was drawn to care for the extremely ill animal.

Finding the sea lion motionless one day, with no apparent breath, and his crusty eyes stuck half open, I flopped him on his belly, flippers outstretched. Kneeling awkwardly over him, I pressed down forcefully, press, release, press, release. It was an improvised sea lion artificial respiration. With a deep rumbling groan, Gus expelled mucus and gave a great wheezing sigh. The next day he shuffled over, dropping his chin in my lap.

Three days later I decided he was well enough to move back outdoors when I discovered him swimming in a four-hundred-gallon display of rock fish. He barked a friendly, innocent, "Hello."

"Have you noticed?" Homer remarked, "Gus only has eyes for you." In his days of delirium and half life, my voice and smell, and will for him to live, made an impression on the young sea lion. I was rewarded with his lasting friendship.

Managing an aquarium was certainly not a desk job. A surprised visitor would sometimes shout, "The seal is loose!" The first time it happened I grabbed a net and ran.

"Hold up, Ted," Homer called, "go easy." Then he showed me how to lead the frightened animal, suddenly in unfamiliar surroundings, gently back into its pool. "Chase an animal into a corner, it might turn mean. You know, it's time you learned a thing or two about these fellows." Homer unbuckled his food caddy and strapped it on my hip. "For starters, the animals have to know you are in command. The food will give you their attention; to earn their respect will take time. Training is just a matter of getting an animal to do what it does naturally, only at the time of the trainer's choosing. Now try this."

Zoom, a new sea lion flew after a tossed fish and hustled back, hamming it up in front of me. "Toss a ring and fish together." The fish was eaten, the floating ring ignored. When I tossed the ring without food the seal investigated, then returned with nothing. Many tries later, Homer said, "Don't give up; toss a fish when he nears the ring. See, he's poking at it; reward him for that. . . . Now he's pushing it, reward him again." After many repetitions, the sea lion finally returned the ring to my hand.

"Homer, how come it took so long? I see him picking up and playing with rings all the time."

"Sure, but you've got to build the association between the ring's return and the reward."

Several months later I began to do some of the regular aquarium shows. At my command the menagerie of seals, sea lions, and Alaska fur seals raced about. The eager, jumping animals splashed the audience, barked continuously, and gathered around their necks as many rings as possible. On stage, I paid them, one fish for each ring collected. I felt they understood the concept; the harder one worked the greater the reward.

Homer recognized that each animal had a personality and said, "You won't find me forcing them into a lock-step routine often seen with trained marine animals. The challenge, Ted, is to keep the show moving, yet allow for their individuality." Giving shows, I watched the audience laugh when they thought I had been outsmarted by a seal. Like my father, a practicing magician in his leisure time, I truly enjoyed rehearsing long hours, developing my "art form," then going on stage. When an audience temporarily forgot they were spectators, and imaginatively put themselves in the position of trainer or even a happy-go-lucky sea mammal, I achieved some of my goal: bringing people to a closer understanding of the marine world. I thought, *a killer whale could have so much impact on those curious to know more, increasing the awareness of millions.*

My fledgling aquarium enterprise thrived with the addition of the performing animal show. After the many visitors had questioned me about teaching sea animals to perform, they responded to my questions. "How many of you have ever seen a killer whale?" I would ask. One or two in each audience indicated the affirmative. When I asked about blackfish, many raised their hands. I tried to clear up the confusion.

Most people, surprised to learn of my interest in the orca whale, said, "But they're so worthless and dangerous; why bother?"

"Think of it," I answered, "how exciting to be next to one, to touch a killer whale, to have one respond to the call of its name."

Many boaters had seen them while cruising Puget Sound and some told me, "Whales are quite a spectacular sight in the wild. I think it would be a shame to confine them in a small pool." A few said, "I would just love to see one close, but is it possible?" Another remarked, "The whales seem unafraid of boats, though they alter course when we follow too closely."

Unprofessional first-hand accounts were plentiful; facts were scarce. Though several hundred orca had been seen at one time, whales are like icebergs, rarely revealing much of themselves. The void of information disappointed me, that no one had a factual understanding of what a whale was all about. I wanted to know: how does an orca think? What is its nature? How would one react to being touched?

Most of my apprehension about approaching an orca in the water stemmed from my concern that it would feel threatened and attack out of fear. "Well, I can't see a killer whale being afraid of YOU," Homer had said. "They have no natural enemies." If Homer was right, I should be able to swim among them without fear.

Commercial fishermen told me they respected the whale's intelligence, cunning, and great strength, but hated them for eating salmon. "How much do you think those blackfish whales eat?" one had asked me.

"I'm not sure, but if they're anything like a seal, they will gobble up the equivalent of five per cent of their body weight every day. A twelve thousand pound orca could consume six hundred pounds or more."

"No wonder there are no fish left!" he raged. "Sometimes that's more than I catch in a couple of days."

"Do orca come near when you have your nets out?"

"Yes, they come right inside the circle, eating all the way."

"What happens then?"

"When we purse-up, they're gone."

"Do they always get away?"

"Once a blackfish stayed too long. We pursed him, but when the netting came aboard, we had a hole just about the size of a whale."

Others told similar stories. Oceanarium-collecting crews captured dolphins and seals in nets, but killer whales apparently could not be contained in them. Searching for new information, I hoped to discover how a killer whale might be approached and captured.

A fan sent me a true story from Australia that illustrates the enigma of the killer whale. During the migrations of the baleen whales, a certain group of orca rushed into Twofold Bay near Eden on the southeast coast of Australia, pounding their tail flukes on the water, creating a thunderous sound. This familiar signal sent the men running to launch their long boats in competition with one another. Pulling hard at the oars, they followed the orca guides out to sea. Soon they came upon a whale already chased to exhaustion. Other orca had previously isolated and ganged up on the great whale, often ripping off big chunks of flesh until they nearly skinned their unfortunate victim alive. It would fall easy prey to the men's harpoon. Lanced and killed, the whale, often a humpback, was left to sink with a buoy attached to the harpoon line. Several days later the bloated carcass surfaced. More of the killer whales' share of the harvest, usually the tongue and lips, had been consumed. The whalers towed their valuable prize to the rendering works. This unique partnership between whale and man reportedly lasted more than one hundred years and is documented in the book, *Killers of Eden* by Tom Mead.

I had previously asked fishing resort and Coast Guard Light Station personnel to call the aquarium collect with any information about killer whales. They had responded occasionally, but I was sure there must be more times when the whales were present in the area. I went out to contact a wider range of people, knocking on the doors of waterfront residents. A typical morning went like this: "Hi, I'm Ted Griffin; I operate the aquarium on the waterfront." The woman's suspicious expression shifted to a friendly smile, as she stood in the doorway of her beach home just north of Seattle. I continued, "I'm looking for a killer whale; do you ever see them?"

"Why yes, now and then. They're such lovely creatures, but aren't they dangerous?"

Another resident with a sweeping view of Puget Sound responded to my inquiry, "You can't be serious? A killer whale in captivity, what if you forgot to feed it?"

And yet another, "Oh yes, they're around quite a lot. Some days they seem to fill the Sound. Won't you have some cookies and tea? Please tell me about your whales."

I spoke of what I had learned so far, correcting misconceptions and answering many questions. Day by day the network of supporters grew, and I gained a real tool in accumulating data. Each time a call came to the aquarium it was logged; when possible, others along the anticipated whale route were notified, and asked to report back. Patterns began to develop.

Social units, called pods, varied in size from three to twenty or more, and always contained a dominant bull. I began to recognize familiar bulls and pod composition. Originally I thought the orca were visitors to Puget Sound, coming from Alaska, Siberia, and even as far away as Japan. Although true for some, the frequent sightings of certain pods throughout the year belied the first concept. "Local" orca rarely, if ever, left the northwest coast of Washington State and British Columbia, Canada; ranging from Puget Sound to Queen Charlotte Sound. The sheltering coastline, with many islands, peninsulas, bays, and coves, and an abundant food supply fills their needs.

At times I followed two or more pods traveling together through Puget Sound. Sometimes the dominant pod bulls swam side by side several miles distant from the main group. If a large, especially noisy freighter approached, the orca quickly regrouped. Some males looked large enough to be the dominant bulls, but with repeated observation I noticed they were less strident than the leaders, their surface time was of shorter duration, the angle of dive sharper, and their course more varied. Pod bulls usually kept their distance from water craft, occasionally lifting their heads for a look around. Once a pod bull became accustomed to the presence of my boat, sometimes taking only a few hours, I often was able to ease alongside him. Frequently he seemed as curious of me as I of him.

I read an account of killer whales' feeding behavior in the Arctic. Hungry orca spread out and visually search along the ice flows for seals, other mammals, or birds. When food is located, whale scouts appear to signal their companions. The intended victim, sensing danger, retreats from the edge, but the whales submerge and break the ice, frightening or dumping their intended prey into the sea. The pursuit is usually brief and bloody. Orca also use teamwork to kill larger whales such as the gray, the blue, the minke, the humpback—all the whales except their own kind. Attacking killer whales hover in rotation directly across a victim's blowhole, preventing breathing. Feeding almost at will, they devour the soft tissues about the mouth of their dying victims, often ripping out the tongue, a reputed orca delicacy, like the whales in Eden, Australia. Commercial whale hunters often speak of taking large whales whose tongue and lips are partially missing. The hapless whale escapes one group of killers and falls prey to another.

I learned that whales were frequently sighted on the Straits of Juan de Fuca near Port Angeles. After driving to the lumber and fishing town on the Olympic Peninsula, I located a fisherman on Edis Hook who offered his boat and time. We went in search of whales every day for three weeks.

A dense morning fog was slow to burn away. We sat silently in the boat, attuned for the sound of a whale's breathing, and heard a whisper of feathers. A seagull, just visible in the mist, settled on the bow, not realizing the boat was occupied. The soft gaggling of feeding ducks suddenly changed to shrill cries. I heard the whistle of many wings. The water's surface erupted with a thunderous roar. Alongside the boat a whale rose—straight up—out of the deep, a minke whale with mouth bulging full. Pushing his tongue like a plunger, the whale forced the water to stream out between the fibrous baleen plates, collecting food in its efficient strainer.

The thirty-foot minke settled back, disappearing below the surface, then unexpectedly rose in the same place.

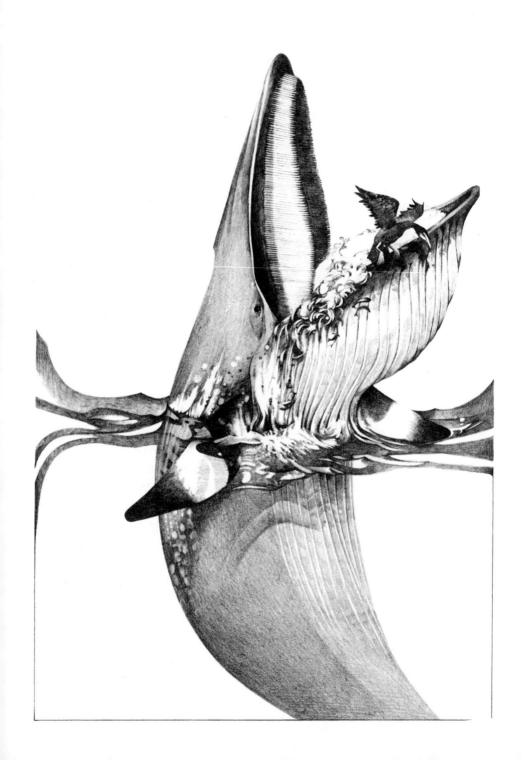

Its mammoth lower jaw dropped full open, expelling a great mass of shiny herring, and, a live, wing-flapping black cormorant! The diving bird, feeding on herring in the whale's path, had been scooped up; surprising the whale as much as the bird.

I recalled how frequently we had encountered sea birds gathered around feeding whales, picking over scraps. This, I thought, was another clue for locating whales.

Though returning to Seattle frustrated, without having sighted orca for the entire three weeks of observation, I imagined the time drawing nearer when I would be close to a killer whale.

Many inquiries led me to the U.S. Fish and Wildlife Service in Seattle (now called N.O.A.A.). I asked a staff biologist at the Marine Mammal Lab how I might capture a killer whale. I was advised that the small-shafted harpoon of the "Greener" gun would cause an orca little injury and he recommended the loan of his department's Greener harpoon-firing rifle.

4
Trial and Error

One beautiful summer day the aquarium received a sighting report and I chartered a helicopter.

In the distance I caught a glimpse, a speck of black. My eyes riveted on the spot. After an eager gesture to the pilot, the helicopter veered to the east, bringing me closer. For a few seconds I thought I saw the dorsal fin of a surfacing whale. Instead a large tree was adrift; an unseen force rolled it again, imparting a semblance of life, standing the fin-shaped root straight out of the water. *I must learn to differentiate what appears alive from that which is alive.* Nearly concealing his wry smile, the pilot returned to our original course without comment.

Bob Rice, wiley veteran Alaskan bush pilot, flew the G-2 Bell helicopter as though an extension of himself. Five hundred feet above Puget Sound, I scanned the surface for orca. To our left the Space Needle towered above the obscuring layers of haze, standing like an unanswered challenge. Glancing down at my feet, I inspected the carefully coiled buoy line, perfect, no snags. If we followed a harpooned whale into a shallow bay, capture might be possible.

We approached the north end of Vashon Island, and watched a half-century old auto ferry pull into the slip. Down the channel two parallel strips of foam marked the path of Pegasus. Pete, my right and left hand man, had rushed off from the aquarium an hour ago, shortly after receiving the whale-sighting report. Pushing the Chrysler-300 engine to the limit, Pete skimmed along at forty knots. I sensed his excitement, the wind in his face, the pungent sea air swelling his lungs, the power of the engine bearing him on.

We were midway along mile-wide Colvos Passage when I shouted to the pilot, "Hold up, look, all across the channel." Was I mistaken again? kelp? ducks? No, killer whales! "Look at them, Bob! There must be fifty or more, at least three pods. They're headed north. We've got to turn them around." In the south of Puget Sound, where I had spent many boyhood days, the shallow, blind bays offered the best opportunity for a whale capture.

How quickly would they sense our presence and react to the throbbing aircraft? As we descended, the broad horizon and rippling green forests gave way to a canyon of tree trunks and high bluffs. Ahead a column of non-conforming glaucous-winged gulls spiraled. Living in perpetual anarchy, the birds dove wildly into a gray mass of herring that boiled at the water's surface. The whales, like shepherds, had driven the nocturnal fish from the depths.

I sagged into my seat, suddenly much heavier, as the pilot pulled out of a steep dive. The nose of our wingless craft rose; we tilted back, mushing to a hover just above the roughened water. I spotted a submerged whale, "There!" Bob Rice pushed the control stick, the helicopter leaped forward. Leaning out the door practically on top of the unsuspecting mammal, I could almost touch him. I wanted to jump from the craft right onto the whale. I watched him rise through the burst of his expired air bubbles. Startled by the hovering craft, the twenty-four-foot whale snapped into a dive. Breaking away in a shallow right turn, he discharged what little breath remained. Now the air-starved mammal had to surface. With a determined second effort the huge animal rose to breathe. His white triangular "saddle" pattern looked familiar. *I know you,* I thought; *I have seen you before.* When he disappeared we searched for more orca; none were visible in the channel. With three fingers I signaled; Bob took us up three hundred feet. In my mind's eye I saw the whales rallying hundreds of feet down in the shadowy, blue-green half light. They located one another using some form of communication. I wished I understood how.

Five minutes later the whales surfaced together, swimming abreast like a cavalry advance. Using the helicopter, we had succeeded in the first step; they were heading south. I cupped my hands around the CB microphone and shouted above the engine roar, "Pete, you pick me up?"

"Roger, Ted. What have you got?"

"Lots of animals, Pete. We're looking good. They're going south, should make Dalco Passage in an hour."

"OK on that. What's your position?"

"Olalla . . . Olalla."

"Roger. I can just make out your flashing beacon. I'll catch up with you in a while."

"Pete, keep well to the rear. Don't overshoot and spook them into turning around. I'll be waiting down the line."

"Got you on that, Ted. I am out."

Point Richmond protrudes into the channel. We circled, searching for a landing site, a place to temporarily stow the passenger door. A spotted harbor seal made his comical belly-sliding dash into the water. He was far from his McNeil Island rookery; I hoped the killers wouldn't interrupt his return home. Bob set the helicopter down close to the beach, reduced power to conserve fuel, and nodded. I stepped out. Shwish—shwish —shwish. I sensed the great energy contained within the spinning rotor blades, but it was an illusion. Now feathered, they accomplished nothing and bled away their potential. Quickly I removed the passenger-side door and anchored it under some rocks, out of the prop wash.

The pilot held out a fistful of straps for me to buckle, then he tugged, checking my safety harness. On previous flights he had insisted on this special seat belt when he learned the door must be removed to clear my shooting path.

I felt the heartbeat of the aircraft in the pulse of the accelerating engine and the throb of rotors as Bob returned them to life. We seemed to levitate off the beach. The nose dipped slightly; we darted out across the channel, steadily gaining altitude. The whale I eagerly sought was once again very near. Dressed in his natural black and white tuxedo, he was like an ambassador from an undersea kingdom.

I regarded the intrepid killer whale as the ultimate animal companion, believing them gentle and sensitive because they nursed and protected their young; yet another side of their personality troubled me, the wolf pack behavior. Unmistakably they are deadly predators. Rather than fear that quality, I viewed their discretionary behavior as indicative of intelligence. For example, they did not instinctively attack skin divers.

Calculating their position and speed while submerged, I imagined myself on their wave length. The roar of the wind whipping past the open cockpit buffered any sound. Bob had to tap my shoulder to interrupt my thoughts. He pointed to the gun at my feet; silent message, *it's time!* I grasped the Greener rifle firmly, careful not to spill the coiled bridle of pay-out line. The lightweight, foot-long harpoon slid snugly over the gas-check barrel. I inserted the gas propellant cartridge into the open breach and took great care closing the lever action; an accidental discharge in the cockpit could send us crashing to our death.

I reviewed each step, visualizing the associated action; I might get only one chance to fire a marker harpoon into an orca. Swinging my right foot outside the cabin, I braced it against the strut, exhaling slowly, releasing tension. I bent over, head between my knees, searching a 360° horizon. Far below us frightened ducks thrashed across the water. Too heavy with food for an airborne escape, they dived. We accelerated, down. I followed Bob's gaze along the west shore. The whales were all together in formation! The stopwatch ticked away the elapsed time of their synchronized dive. I had learned they would surface to breathe three times, at fifteen second intervals, then all disappear.

"They're up!" I shouted with uncontrolled excitement, but the wind ate my words. We raced for our rendezvous, still out of range on their second breath. I counted the final seconds. Our only chance was following the progressive circles of turbulent water in the wake of a shallow-diving whale. Four seconds . . . five . . . six. It was up to Bob; he had to position me directly over a whale the exact moment it surfaced. I leaned out the door, buffeted by the wind. My body was taut, straining to the limit of the harness, rifle pressed firmly to my shoulder. Safety? Off! Line? Clear! Ready . . . ten . . . eleven. We were right over a dozen animals. The dorsal fin of the pod bull slowly broke the surface, his speed steady, seemingly unconcerned with our ominous presence. I aimed for the thick blubber area on the whale's left flank. He was out of range. Thirteen . . . fourteen. "Bob!" but he couldn't see the whale. I waved frantically, *My way! My way!* Fifteen . . . sixteen—I fired—boom.

The shiny projectile flew out, straight for the target, white nylon line streaming behind, rifle report lost in the wind. "I hit the whale!" To my surprise the bull continued forward, his swimming behavior unaltered. I felt a momentary remorse at shooting him, even with this smallest of missiles, yet it was the only way I thought it possible to capture a killer whale.

Absorbed in watching the giant orca, I forgot to pay attention to the buoy line that stretched between the whale and our helicopter. Suddenly the craft dropped sharply to starboard. The line was drum tight. The buoy was caught near my feet, too late to throw it out. The helicopter was falling from the sky; the diving whale was dragging us to our doom! I fumbled for my pocket knife in near panic but couldn't reach it. TWANG! The snagged buoy suddenly broke free and flew out the open copter door, disappearing underwater. Instantly Bob recovered the falling craft; I fought immobilizing shock. With intense concentration I focused on the last two buoys and the attached line, tossing them all out the door; catastrophe was averted.

When I could draw a breath I glanced at Bob. The burden of responsibility for the near disaster weighed heavily on me. The look in his eyes told me how close to death we had come. In his faint smile there was the sign of his own tremendous relief. With the slight nod of his head I gained the expression I sought, *It's all over, Ted; you must forget it.*

I signaled, *all clear*, and we began a rapid ascent. As always, Bob established sufficient altitude to accommodate an emergency glide to the nearest shore. My attention rocketed back to the red buoys, tied on the harpoon line. They marked the whale's direction of travel. The animal swam with ease, buoys in tow, at seven knots or more, faster than the killer whales usually cruise.

Fourteen minutes elapsed before the orca reappeared. "That is the longest dive I've ever seen," I said to Bob. The first two marker buoys did not resurface. I guessed they had collapsed under immense water pressure hundreds of feet down.

The swiftly-moving whales skimmed along just below the surface, remaining visible between the three breath intervals. When their blood was replenished with oxygen, they vanished.

The orca approached Dalco Passage right on schedule. I expected Pete to appear any moment. I might need him. A slight gritch nagged at my thoughts; would they continue south into lower Puget Sound? Reviewing various whale-capture possibilities, I reasoned, with "Griffin" logic, how each option held some promise of success. I would get the big bull tired and tow him ashore, or block his retreat from the shallows and let the fifteen-foot change in tide strand him. Failing all else, I was prepared to leap from the helicopter onto a whale's back and loop a rope around its tail!

A cluster of small kicker boats trolled near Point Defiance in Dalco Passage, criss-crossing, vying for position. Blackmouth salmon concentrated there year around. Many of the fisherfolk regarded the salmon-eating whales as their sworn enemies. I hoped no one would notice the bull and shoot him.

Just north of Gig Harbor I spotted many plumes of white mist rising from the water. The surfacing whales, after repeated dives of long duration, expired air with great force. For a while they all lolled about, offering no indication of their next move. An uneasiness crept over me. Three bulls converged offshore, away from the main pod; among them swam the one I sought, harpoon shaft visible in his left flank. Odd, why were just bulls lingering at the surface? Two whales inspected the harpoon protruding from the third animal.

When Pegasus came into sight, I called on the radio, "Pete, do you read me?"

Pegasus slowed to an idle; Pete answered, "Roger, Ted."

"OK, we're in good shape. Let's figure they'll continue south under the Narrows Bridge, but just in case they have other ideas, guard their eastern escape route. Shut down in Dalco between the ferry docks and watch for a break-out around Vashon Island."

"I've got you, Ted; I'm on my way." The bow of Pegasus rose momentarily, then leveled out as Pete accelerated to planing speed. The boat leaped over the wake of a lumbering houseboat-cruiser, tossing great plumes of spray to either side.

The buoy skipped along in a southerly direction toward the Narrows, then slowed and stopped. Darn, the whales seemed undecided. A short while ago the tide had turned; now the current was running north out of the Narrows against the whales. Thirteen . . . fourteen . . . fifteen minutes passed. The buoy remained motionless. Had the bull shaken off the harpoon and given us the slip?

The quiet waters of the bay were suddenly RIPPED apart. The whales burst to the surface in a row, extending from shore to shore. They plunged forward, with each stride clearing the water like porpoise, charging directly toward Pete. The towed buoy leaped ahead in a towering cascade of spray, keeping pace with the onrushing bull. Passing Point Defiance, the orange buoy raised havoc among the fishermen.

"Pete," I yelled into the CB, "you see 'em?"

"See them? You must be kidding!"

"Get on them, Pete."

"Where do I begin?"

"Anywhere. Make a run, cut 'em off. You've got to stop them from getting out of the Sound."

"I'll give it a try, Ted, but oh boy I've never seen them so steamed up."

Two jets of trapped water burst from Pegasus' exhaust ports. I could almost hear the deep rumble of the

accelerating engine. Running full speed, the boat closed fast. Pete had to reach the escaping whales before they took a second breath, then they would likely turn the other direction to breathe.

A rising dorsal fin gave Pete the needed position check. Pegasus rushed on toward a wall of surfacing whales. "No! Don't ram them!" I shouted. At the last possible moment Pete turned away, yards short of the lead whales. Frantically they tried to stop in mid-flight, spilling over each other like Jackstraws. The half-mile-long row of whales dove simultaneously as though each believed it was on a collision course with the one boat. Those whales hundreds of yards away were in no danger of hitting Pegasus, yet they exhibited the same fear of collision, and behaved the same, as those that thought they were in danger. I could see black and white underbellies as they rolled and faded into the depths. Some of the orca had been unable to make air, just as we planned. Their oxygen depleted, they would need to surface immediately. Pete circled back toward his starting point, criss-crossing the channel, creating a sound barrier to frighten the whales.

The winded mammals surfaced to breathe, and with great resolve set a northeasterly course, undeterred by Pete's continuing efforts. Since they were headed north out of Puget Sound, I chose to cut my losses and reluctantly motioned to the pilot; the expensive copter would be sent back. I would follow the whales in the boat, hoping they might again turn south.

We made a brisk, low-level pass, alerting Pete, then headed toward Vashon Island's south shore. Bob landed on a deserted stretch of tree-lined beach. Loaded with equipment I stepped out and stood clear. He waved, "Good luck," and lifted off.

All was quiet . . . yet I continued to experience the sensation of wind and pulsating rotor blades. Sitting on a log I allowed myself this precious time alone to relax. Employing a technique which was second nature to me, I visualized a fast-running river. The tension I had built up all through the day began to flow away. Too soon Pete arrived.

I clambered aboard and, taking the controls, backed Pegasus off the beach. CRUNCH! Oh no, the boat had hit a rock. Pete picked up the boat-hook and poled us to deeper water, remarkably restraining himself from comment. Cautiously revving the engine I discovered the propeller had a considerable vibration. Pete shrugged, "You want to stop and put on the spare?"

"No, we'd lose them," I answered in a quiet, strained voice; "I'll just hold it down."

"OK, but maybe something's going to fly loose."

I nodded acknowledgement, unable to muster further words, and tried to overtake the rapidly-moving marker buoy. Like unbridled horses on an infinite prairie, the spirited whales took their head. I envied their freedom to roam the oceans, masters of their destinies. My dream of holding one captive, for interaction, was a paradox.

An hour passed. The wounded Pegasus throbbed. I had to slow that whale down. "Pete, the sea anchor, is it aboard?"

"Yes, forward."

"Let's give it a try."

Pete rigged the three-foot-diameter canvas funnel, which resembled an aircraft windsock. We barely overtook the marker float behind the whale. By watching the run of the white harpoon line in the water, I could maintain slack. Pete lifted the last buoy and attached the tow bridle for the anchor. Positioning the cone, he released his hold when the nylon line drew taut. Exerting a drag force of about one thousand pounds, it was pulled briskly away, the great orca's departure from Puget Sound unaltered. How could he do it? What stamina! Later I realized it was a fairly small load relative to his body size.

With the approach of darkness, Pete fastened a marker light atop a small styrofoam kickboard, securing it behind the towed buoy. Our miniature whale-boat zipped smartly along like a toy pulled by a child, its light dancing in the darkness, denoting the northward progress of the large mammal.

A small point of light crossed the sky, too bright and fast-moving for a star. Then a wall of blackness loomed ahead, shutting off the world. It seemed to be over us like an envelope. A large freighter passed very near! Had it sunk us, probably no one would have known. A surge of adrenalin momentarily boosted my sagging spirits.

Another hour drifted away. Directly abeam to starboard a white light flashed every five seconds, Alki Point. Just around the corner were Elliot Bay and Seattle. The changing tide was my last hope. The shift in current might induce the whales to reverse direction.

"Pete," I yawned, "you might as well get some sleep. It looks like a long night."

The little light stopped moving. "Hey, Ted, do you think the whales are changing direction?"

"I hope so! It's about time things started going our way. We can still do it, Pete. They could reach lower Sound by daybreak if they've really turned south."

I stopped the boat fifty yards from the kickboard light, its only movement caused by a slight lapping of wave, and wondered, *What is the big devil up to?* More minutes passed, curiosity was driving me wild. I eased the boat closer. The whale could double back and foul the harpoon line in the propeller. As a precaution Pete reached out with the boat hook, and picking up the rope, brought light-sled, buoy, and sea-anchor aboard. Gingerly he began to haul in some of the one-thousand-foot line.

"Shhh, Pete, can you hear the whale's breathing?"

"No."

"There. What was that?"

"Wishful thinking," was Pete's laconic reply.

Taking turns, we pulled in yard after yard of the nylon line, coiling it into a laundry basket, ready to pay out again when the whale made his run. My fingers tingled in anticipation of the line being stripped from them.

"He must be right under us, Pete. If he rammed us, he'd smash the plywood hull."

There was no thrilling tug. When I held a badly-bent harpoon in my hand, reality forced me to admit it was over. I groped for a flashlight. In the bright beam I saw the snap-out barbs twisted over, rendering the harpoon useless.

"Do you want to try and find them again tonight?" asked Pete.

I did, desperately, but said instead, "No, we wouldn't have a chance. They're wise to us."

Pegasus rounded Alki Point. On the horizon the Space Needle appeared graceful and radiant. The sight lifted my spirits. I felt if others could conceive of such an idea and overcome the problems of building it, I could fulfill my dream. Closing my eyes I saw that bull again and again, his dorsal fin hooked left with a rippled trailing edge. I would recognize him, and next time . . . .

Although each whale-capture trip had ended in failure, I remained certain a solution existed. I needed more facts and more frequent opportunities to study them. Out prospecting for whale spotters, I interrupted a conversation among fishermen, "What kind of whales did you see?"

"Killer whales. Blackfish. They ought to bomb all them dumb whales out of here, use them for target practice. They're nothing but a nuisance," one answered.

"What did they look like?" I asked. "Are you sure they were killers?"

"Them was killers all right. Those bloody devils! I cracked one good with my ought-six. Hit him solid, heard the slug smack into him. Never stopped him though. That big, black fin standing in the air, he just kept a coming steady, like he owned the world. Naw, the fishing ain't gonna be no good for awhile."

I felt faint, his realism so vivid I could almost feel the bullet ripping into *my* body. A flood of emotion swept me. Having a strong affinity for the whales, I anguished over their plight.

Many people regarded the killer whale as little different from sharks, though possibly more dangerous. For some fishermen, blasting away at whales was considered a harmless pastime, even useful to their occupation. I believed that behavior wrong, but could not pass judgment. Others had accused me of maliciously chasing whales. They lumped me with the fishermen, commercial whalers, and big game hunters. The fact that I sought the killer whale alive, believing it intelligent, sensitive, and capable of interaction with humans, made little difference to them. I wanted to have others see the whales as I did, but misinformation abounded. Facts, on which to build a rational understanding of the animals, were almost nonexistent.

A month later a phone call came to the aquarium. Pete said, "Ted, it's the captain of the Bremerton ferry on the ship-to-shore."

I listened to the fellow's information and responded, "A pod of whales headed south. Thanks, skipper. I'll go have a look." Slamming down the phone with my usual excitement, I shouted, "Pete. The whales I saw yesterday must have turned around and come back. I'm going after them."

Catching up with the mammals near Vashon Island, I caught sight of a blue helicopter circling overhead, then, a man leaning out the open door. I could hardly believe someone else was following the whales! In an emotional outburst I raced Pegasus to a position just below the hovering aircraft, waved my arms and bellowed,

"YOU GET AWAY FROM MY WHALES!"

"YOUR WHALES, you say?" he shouted back, "you'll have to catch them first!"

I flushed with the realization that I had acted like a rancher possessive of his herd. The fellow leaning from the cockpit was Don Goldsberry from the Tacoma Municipal Aquarium. The significance of our encounter was not lost. I later asked him to work for me, but that day the whales left us both empty handed.

5
Call of the Whales

A few days later I was cruising Puget Sound in a helicopter. Two bull orca swam just below the surface. I had seen the rest of their pod nearly three miles away and had sent Pete over in the boat to keep track of them. In unison the two bulls slowly swung their heads from side to side in wide arcs without altering speed or direction. Simultaneous streams of bubbles emanated from their blowholes.

The radio crackled with Pete's excited voice, "They're moving out, changing direction." In Pegasus he had followed the cows and calves on a course parallel to ours.

"What's their new heading?" I asked.

"Roughly northwest."

"OK, Pete. . . . Hey, the bulls are also changing direction. They're going northwest as well."

The bulls must have been in communication with the others, but how did they do it across three miles? Several hours later the two bulls, on an intersecting course, merged with the pod.

Recent studies have shown orca can signal one another over a distance of at least five miles.

Another day the wind was howling out of the south at around forty knots, the waves in the narrow inlet six feet high. Working my way up to little Herron Island, I spotted an entire pod of whales in the lee, the island's north shore. On other occasions, when the whales seemed to vanish in stormy weather, I often could relocate them by searching the protected side of each landfall.

When the pod departed, I raced forward in Pegasus, overtaking them in south Puget Sound. One-half mile ahead I stopped, waiting for their approach. I was thrilled when a cow swam toward me, passing within a few yards. When she was some distance off I started the engine. Seeing no other whales I turned toward her, but had to speed up when she increased her pace. She porpoised every fifteen seconds, leaping out of the big waves as though in effortless flight. I could just keep pace with her at 3,500 rpm, about thirty knots. The hull was pounding in the heavy seas. It was unusual not seeing the rest of her pod, but I remained with her, my only lead.

Suddenly she was gone. I stopped and scanned the horizon, looking and listening. I never saw another whale that day. I concluded she had deliberately led me away when the same thing happened on several more occasions, in just the same fashion, always by a cow. The whales were definitely skillful in the decoy business.

During rough weather it was difficult to follow whales in a boat as they were frequently concealed between the waves when surfacing. Often my only clue to their location was the bull's tall dorsal fin. Catching sight of the "black flag" on one occasion I accelerated the engine and sped in his direction. Nearing the big orca, I saw him rise ten feet above the water and take a long look at me. For the next hour I lost sight of the bull until by chance he surfaced near my drifting craft. I did not see him, only heard a familiar blowing sound. In fifteen seconds he breathed again, but his dorsal fin was not visible. Laying on his side as he surfaced, he had lifted his head to breathe. On his third breath he repeated the dorsal-concealing behavior. In the period of an hour he had recognized that I was chasing the sight of his fin. I believe he made an association between the timing of his appearance and my revving the engine. I soon lost sight of the animals and had to give up following them. When other orca used the same evasive behavior, I was intrigued with their intelligence, and had to modify my approach-follow tactics.

On a hot day in late August excited boaters gathered around a pod of feeding whales just outside Seattle's Government Locks. The orca did not seem to be upset with all the craft maneuvering close to them. I could hear the viewers' oooohs and aaaahs as the whales frolicked.

A six-foot newborn calf followed closely alongside its mother. Previous observations had convinced me that the wrinkled, sometimes reddish skin was a clue to orcas' young age. A few months after their birth, generally during February-March-April, the non-black skin areas lose the redness, becoming orange, then yellow, and within the year, white.

I stood on the bow of Pegasus and watched for familiar fin shapes and saddle patterns. These distinctions are as unique to whales as nose and eye shapes to humans.

Late in the day I crossed the Sound, tagging along with the same pod. When the mammals took a straight-line course, I was able to get ahead of them and stop. The smaller animals were curious and swam toward my boat, diving at the last moment, then surfacing just beyond. I put the engine in gear to ease alongside the shallow-diving youngsters. They crossed under Pegasus' bow swimming upside down, in a row with heads aligned. Soon I was surrounded by the pod of fifteen or so, and we traveled together for a few minutes. They sounded; the pod bull cut across my path. As he dove, his flukes popped once. Was he saying good-bye, or stay away?

When the sun left the sky, the air became moist and dense, more readily carrying their breathing sounds which guided me in the darkness. I was haunted by the whales' eerie calls and short bursts of sonar clicks, reaching my ears through the hull of Pegasus. Puget Sound was without a ripple, but below its tranquil surface the age-old struggle between life and death continued. A torpedo-shaped, iridescent glow, like that of Captain Nemo's submarine Nautilus, grew brighter and brighter, heading straight for me at ramming speed. The bizarre sight was enthralling. The eerie blue-green outline of a salmon streamed under my boat, a pursuing whale overtook and engulfed the panicked prey. I heard the sharp crack of a dorsal slap. As if in answer came the distant popping of pectoral fins.

Small luminous marine organisms, set astir by contact with whales and fish, momentarily gave off light. The darting fish created a marine "meteor shower", whales looked like fireballs. A cow passed with a tiny calf perfectly outlined, swimming inches higher than mother. "Flying" together with such precision, they appeared linked. I could make out a mother's whistle, a calf's answer with little quick squeals. The chattering sounds were melodious. Some whales seemed to be communicating over great distances, while others hummed to themselves. The slow rhythmic pulse of one orca's long-range sonar sounded like the creaking of an old wooden bridge when a loaded truck passes over. Finding a target the whale shifted to a burst of rapid clicks, then was silent. I felt I understood them; I was one of them.

After midnight a fresh breeze just off Point No Point covered the sounds of my animal friends, leaving me with a deep loneliness. Later the air became still, with no boat engines, cars, trains, airplanes, no sounds, none. In many years of boating I had never experienced such a time. I dared not move, fearing I'd break the sublime silence. Listening for the whales in total darkness, all senses heightened, I opened my mouth, stopped breathing and turned my head slowly. There? I swallowed and stretched my jaw, ears crinkled slightly and cleared. I thought I could hear them, faintly.

I slept a while and dreamed of a mythical whale who beckoned, "I dare you; cast aside your preconceptions of me. Does it frighten you, my killing sea lions for sport and gray whale for supper? What do you really know of my life? Do not be misled by those who fear me, theirs is a limited world. Heed the advice of caution and be denied your opportunity to join me."

I awoke and looked skyward to get my bearings. I saw shooting stars; they were like a celebration. One . . . five, six, . . . ten, that one is manmade; oh why not? eleven.

With the coming dawn, the brightest stars disappeared one by one. The whales, too, had vanished. For a long time darkness continued upon the sea and the land; all was gray and indistinguishable. I felt an unnatural, unaccountable loneliness, as though suspended, caught between two thoughts, two places, two times.

In the next weeks I was often aware of that night on Puget Sound. With little conscious effort I rejected any persons unable or unwilling to support my inevitable association with a killer whale. I actively sought only those individuals who concurred with my ultimate success. With all the power and emotional force of a Rachmaninoff Concerto I vividly experienced my goal as already achieved. I saw myself alongside the whale. My hand was sliding over his smooth, firm body. He held steady. I mounted his back. I drew a deep breath. The water rushed by. I was astride the mighty behemoth heading into another world.

6
In Debt

By mid-September tourist traffic along the waterfront was minimal. To pass the time on slow days I joined my neighbor on the pier, Captain Lynn Campbell, aboard his harbor tour vessel now only half full of visitors, for the one-hour cruise around Elliott Bay. I scanned the horizon for whales and listened to Lynn's narration. Seattle's history came alive. He excited me with his tales of four-masted schooners sailing with cargoes of gold and lumber. I liked most the story of the early pioneers who had risked everything to gain their freedom, and a slim chance for wealth in this new land of opportunity.

Lynn closed his tour business for the winter. The fish and animals had to be fed and cared for so I kept the aquarium open. The whale-capture attempts had depleted my cash reserves. Poor winter attendance added to my money problem. On several occasions my brother had asked about the growing seriousness of my financial condition, but I was avoiding the issue. Finally Jim confronted me, "Ted! You are in real trouble. Any one of your creditors could force you into bankruptcy."

Our roles had become reversed. I was taller than Jim, a year older, and always had thought of myself as his big brother. He had earned a degree in business from Stanford and became a successful entrepreneur in a variety of ventures. The serious, mature expression on his handsome, boyish face seemed incongruous as he sternly laid out what I must do.

When I resisted the recommended restrictions on my

free-wheeling style, he snapped, "Do you think I take pleasure in this? I'm your brother. No one else is going to help you. There are no free rides in this world. One way or another, we all work for everything in life. Even the air isn't free. You have to breathe to get it." Jim's anger quickly melted into a little smile. I felt a strong resentment for what I considered his interference, and at myself for getting into the predicament. I applied for a bank loan which Jim guaranteed, then arranged rent deferment, laid off most of the aquarium employees, and reluctantly promised I would curtail whale-capture attempts.

It was a difficult time. I was often at the aquarium alone with my "watchdogs", the seals in the front pool. They began barking the moment a visitor entered. I couldn't afford to heat the building and some days found ice on the floor under a leaking fish tank. I wore my diving suit all day since I was cold and in water so much. Each time City Light threatened to disconnect the power, I pleaded, "All the fish and animals will die." They allowed another extension. Joan came to sell tickets on the busier weekends.

In the Spring a turn in my finances came in an unexpected way. An offer of two Alaskan fur seal pups rescued by fishermen from Puget Sound, increased my awareness of the value of publicity. One look at the nearly-dead sacks of flesh, fur, and bones in a garbage pail and I couldn't refuse. The babies quickly thawed under a twenty-four-hour heat-lamp. After several weeks of good food and vitamins, they grew fat and sassy, but I was off my budget. Having them healthy again, however, was worth many times the cost. A photograph appeared in the *Seattle Times* newspaper of the "father" holding his "twins". The human-interest story of the orphaned fur seal pups brought an overwhelming number of aquarium visitors.

Jim was pleased to learn attendance was ahead of projections, but hearing my expenses were up, he cautioned, "Remember our agreement; don't buy anything new. Keep within your budget no matter how much it hurts, then you'll make it."

Joan asked again, "When can you take a small salary?"

"I don't know, but if the first-rate attendance continues, then maybe soon." Food was always on the table and the home mortgage paid by Joan. She managed to support our family of two adults and two babies from some mysterious reserves. I later learned they came from previous planning and good budgeting. I was grateful for her wonderful help.

One morning a slightly-built man about my age stepped to the ticket counter. His business, he said, was advertising and public relations. I was very interested, but told him I had no money to pay for his services. He offered to cover his expenses until my income increased. As things turned out, it was one of the best bargains I made at the aquarium. The two of us came up with many ideas which increased attendance, and I very soon could pay his fee.

At one of our promotions, "COME SEE PUGET SOUND'S MOST FEARSOME CREATURE," I spotted the familiar face of a diving friend.

"Hello, Dell, haven't seen you lately. How did you hear about all this?"

"Gary told me you needed help and to get right over."

"Good, come on around back and give me a hand."

Grabbing hold of my giant "fishlines," we each gave a strong tug. Dell said, "I can't pull this rope up; must be fouled."

"Are you willing to put on a wet suit and go under the pier for a look?"

"Lead the way, Ted."

Each following a rope, we "walked" hand over hand,

down, down, sixty, seventy, eighty feet. In the subdued light something moved. Suddenly I was confronted by the jaws of a large shark! With a frightful chill I recalled smacking into something solid under the pier the night I struggled with the octopus.

"Dell!" I shouted into my regulater, but my diving companion was six feet away grappling with a second "mud shark" which was grinding its multi-rows of razor sharp teeth on the chain leader. I motioned, *Open the shark's jaw.* He wrapped his legs around the torso of the twelve-foot-long critter and pulled back on its snout. The teeth parted; I pried out the huge hook. Free of the tether, the shark struggled to get away, but Dell remained astride the thrashing creature, grasping its sandpaper-like skin. As the snapping shark lunged, I swung on behind Dell. Visibility approached zero in the stirred-up mud. The shark's swinging tail propelled us right along. Dell looked over his shoulder at me, only inches away. With eyes sparkling, he was laughing so hard his mask partially filled with water. We knew it was really dangerous, but too much fun to give up. He steered the shark by pulling the snout; we circled slowly upward. Breaking the water's surface I heard a reporter shout, "Are you two fellows crazy?" Yes, crazy enough to have gone back underwater and ridden the second shark up.

It was a smashing success; broke all attendance records, got a big photograph and write-up in the papers, and TV coverage. Those two sharks and a smaller one caught from my boat earlier became a popular exhibit at the aquarium. Because of their light-sensitive eyes, mud sharks come into shallow water only at night. I guessed a fish-processing operation on the next pier must have attracted them.

My press agent had recognized how something in all of us shudders and screams at the mention of sharks;

they're sinister and dangerous. He suggested however, that greater than a fear of the beast is the curiosity of it. This was borne out by the visitors' reactions. Fear both attracted and repelled them, but once near the creature, fear faded, and their interest and questions were endless.

Several weeks later Jim stopped by for one of his regular visits from Tacoma. I filled him in on the recent events.

"You made it, Ted? Your creditors, the bank, they're all paid off?"

"Yes, Jim, I can hardly belive it myself. It's just been six months since I received the fur seal pups."

"I saw another story about your aquarium in the paper. How do you do it?"

"Oh, it's Gary Boyker's work. You remember him, that publicity fellow you nearly didn't let me hire."

7
Moby Doll

Joan's dark-brown hair streamed in the wind as we "flew" north in Pegasus, skipping across the choppy water, munching peanut butter and honey sandwiches. With spirits high, we entered the Vancouver, B.C. harbor and searched along the shoreline. A pier enclosed with a fence drew my attention. Signs said, "Danger," "No Trespassing." Undeterred, we tied the boat and climbed the long barnacle-encrusted ladder.

"Do you suppose this is the place?"

"Maybe she's been moved."

"No, look down there. Someone's tied a few lingcod through the mouth so they'll stay alive."

A fin broke the surface of the muddy water. A fifteen-foot killer whale drew a shallow breath, and sank out of sight. To get closer I climbed down to a small float inside the enclosure; the whale circled by. Surely the animal wanted to make friends. Starry-eyed expectation soon faded into disappointment. The whale looked gaunt, skin pocked without a sheen, its movements lethargic. Though I couldn't see the eyes I sensed they were lifeless. In light of the whale's traumatic capture, it was pure folly to have expected anything else.

In the Canadian Gulf Islands men had waited several months, tending their shore-mounted whalers' gun. The Vancouver Public Aquarium had wanted a dead orca to copy for a full-scale plastic replica. When a killer whale swam close enough, they had fired; the three-foot-long, steel harpoon passed right through, above the spine. A newspaper account told how companion whales had come to the harpooned animal's rescue, supporting it until recovered from shock. Tethered on the stout harpoon line, the injured mammal was led fifty miles across the Straits of Georgia into Vancouver harbor. At first housed in a submerged drydock, it resided in a pier-pen at the time of our visit.

Joan called out, "Why don't you try feeding her?"

I gripped the head of a wiggling, two-foot fish and slapped its tail on the water. The orca was momentarily startled, having just surfaced, then resumed its methodical swimming pattern. I tried again, slapping the fish until the animal swam closer. Undulating the cod back and forth underwater, I called, "Come on there, fellow, come to me." The whale, named "Moby Doll" by her captors, headed directly my way, but at three yards she hesitated, then turned slowly. She had to be very hungry; I saw no empty strings among the tied fish. Perhaps she was too weak to eat. The second time, splashing the water lured the whale close enough to stroke her nose with the fish. The animal's jaw opened, revealing forty or so yellowish, conical teeth. I cautioned her, "Just the fish, not the hand that feeds you." Ever so gently the food was tugged away. A rush came over me; at last, contact with a whale! "Wheeeeeeerree," I whistled to her each time she circled past. Placing another fish in the water and repeating the splashing sequence brought the animal from across the enclosure. Uncertain if she ate the first fish, I clearly saw her swallow the second. Like a lost child finding a friend in a strange environment, the young whale waited. "Do you want another cookie?" She needed to be hugged, loved; I thought of taking her home. In fact, I wanted Moby Doll so much I considered stealing her.

"Ted!" Joan's voice conveyed alarm. "Company's coming."

Terribly disappointed I rushed up the ladder. From a distance I recognized the director of the Vancouver Public Aquarium. "You're doing a naughty thing," he began.

"The whale is eating, Murray, right out of my hand."

He maintained his reserve; my success in feeding Moby Doll unacknowledged, but of course I never expected the unauthorized visit to merit a warm reception. I realized he probably felt as possessive of his whale as I would have. Joan and I departed, certain at least the whale would welcome our return.

Unfortunately Moby Doll succumbed to her injuries and died the following month. The autopsy revealed the orca to be an adolescent male. Though Moby Doll lived but a short time in captivity and was never on display in the Vancouver Aquarium, she nevertheless created considerable interest in whales. Many, many people wanted a closer inspection, and further knowledge of the killer whales so prevalent in British Columbia waters.

For the next few months I searched for whales with the trio from Portland. In February we went all out, chartering commercial fishing vessels and numerous aircraft. The massive effort began to pay off; we got one orca on a line. Bob and I were confident of imminent success. He announced to the press that a whale was caught. We struggled three days in biting-cold weather and heavy seas to get the animal aboard; expenses mounted by the hour. When the whale broke free I was terribly disappointed, but so exhausted I actually felt relieved the ordeal had ended.

In the aftermath, I felt the frustration of repeated failure. For three years every attempt to catch a live killer whale had fallen short. I considered giving up the quest. Again I owed money to many people. In sympathy with my dream, they extended the deadlines. When I looked for a new solution, I found none. Yet the strength to continue came from the vision of that brief encounter with Moby Doll.

8
The Wild Card

All winter long I could think only of whales, hating to leave the phone for fear of missing a report. I jumped at shadows, once driving all night to the northwest corner of the state to investigate a vague whale sighting at Neah Bay. Another day I flew to the San Juan Islands. Leaping out of the float plane I thoroughly mystified a clam digger by running across the beach and asking, "Have you seen any whales?"

In frustration I snapped at aquarium employees, rarely said "Hello," considered nearly everyone an obstacle, had no time for anything except whales, and was told more than once I was impossible to be around.

Like a compulsive gambler I often said, "Just one more card, just one more chance, I'll win this time," but my money was gone. I thought I would die if the search had to stop.

One cool June evening, Joan and I were up late talking about the children, the aquarium, if I would ever take a vacation, and mostly about our future. She didn't mention the time spent looking for whales. Joan wasn't a complainer; I think she felt my obsession would run itself out. The ringing phone interrupted our conversation. "Who would be calling at this time of night?" Joan asked.

"May I speak with Ted Griffin, please?"

"Speaking."

"Are you the fellow who owns the aquarium?"

"Yes."

"My name is Walter Piatocka. I have two killer whales

68

for sale."

"KILLER WHALES! Are you sure?"

"No doubt about it."

"Alive? Where? How have you got them? I mean, how are you holding them?"

"In nets."

"IN NETS? Are they tangled? They must be injured."

"No. They're perfectly all right."

"Where are they?"

"In Warrior Cove, near a little cannery town north of Vancouver Island. Do you know Port Hardy?"

"Yes—yes."

"It's about seventy-five miles north of there."

"That's five-hundred miles from here. How do I drive there?"

"You can't. Boat or plane."

"What are you asking for the whales?"

"Come up and make an offer, but you better come quick or they'll be sold to someone else." Click.

I was numb. *Finally, whales, but hundreds of miles away, in a foreign country. At any moment they could escape, die, be sold to someone else: Marineland? Vancouver Aquarium? The Portland group? They all have the money, manpower, expertise.* Joan interrupted my thoughts, "Ted, how would you get two whales back to Seattle?"

"I don't know, Joan, but I have to go, at least see them. There might even be a way to buy them."

"Where will you get the money?"

"Maybe I can pay the fishermen when I get the whales home, earn the money from putting them on display."

"It's not likely they'll go for a deal like that, especially if they know the state of your finances. But I know you won't rest until you make the trip. Go. I'll manage the aquarium while you're away."

9
The Gamble

In June of 1965 the skipper of a purse seiner one day out of Ketchikan, Alaska, overheard a ship-to-ship communication. He radioed his companion on another fishing vessel, "Adam, you pick up on those Canadian fishermen talking about killer whales? . . . Seems a gill netter had to cut his net loose in that storm last night because it had drifted onto some rocks. Later the net trapped a couple of whales. Sounds like they're looking for some outfit to take them off their hands."

"Chinook back. Yeah, Pete, I got you on that. Maybe they haven't heard about that Griffin fellow in Seattle."

"Pacific Maid back. Probably not. I think I'll give the fishermen a call."

We were cleared through Canadian customs at remote Bedwell Harbor in the Gulf Islands and several hours later landed at Alert Bay for fuel. My stomach was tied in knots; I chatted aimlessly with my companion, Gary Boyker.

"This is it, boys." Our pilot pointed to the isolated settlement, an assortment of red roofs, bunkhouses, large commercial buildings, and piers, linked by wooden walkways. We touched down in the quiet harbor with a backdrop of green mountains disappearing into a low-hanging mist.

A bespeckled man in plaid shirt and stubble beard sprang to catch the plane wing, turning us parallel to the float. "Hello there," he said, sizing us up in our business suits. "You must be here to see the whales. I'm Paul Thomas, 'stringing' for *National Geographic*."

He introduced Gary and me to the whales' captors who asked us to come aboard their gillnetter. "We'll run you out there. It's just a couple of miles."

On the trip to Warrior Cove I asked one of them, "Why don't they break through your net?"

"Oh that bothered us all right. We added two more; I hope it's enough."

"And that's all you have to hold them?"

"Well, yes, they've been in there three days now."

Suddenly the gillnet boat heeled over, whirled around and headed back, without slowing. "What? Why aren't we going to see the whales?" I asked.

One fisherman spoke to the other, "We're not wasting any more time with these two."

Gary turned to me with an expression of utter hopelessness, "I was explaining how you planned to pay for the whales with a letter of credit. He didn't seem to understand, became very upset, saying Marineland is coming to buy the whales with cash. Also he expects to sell for considerably more than you and I discussed."

Close to tears, searching for the right words, I confronted one of the whales' captors on the cannery wharf, "I want a killer whale more than you can imagine. It's my lifelong ambition. If for any reason you are unable to find a buyer please phone me anytime, day or night, collect; here is my number." I pressed a card into his powerful hand. "Call me; I will come immediately, with cash." I held the focus of his eyes with mine, and repeated silently, *remember me; I'm the one you will call. You will call me; you will call; you must call.*

Airborne, I saw a long string of white net-floats partly blocking a cove. A portion of gillnet was snagged on a reef in the cove's center, forming a small enclosure. I turned to the pilot, "Vickery, take us down. This must be Warrior Cove."

Whoosh. Whoosh. Two whales surfaced just outside the enclosed area. "Oh, they've escaped!" The two whales pressed their chins against the corkline; then I realized they were a cow and calf, only curious visitors. Inside the nets a black fin broke the surface like a submarine periscope. It rose, oscillating back and forth. The bull orca, roughly twenty-four feet long, took a breath, but did not submerge. An eight to ten foot calf popped up, swimming with ease, and began rubbing on the larger whale. The bull slowly settled out of sight. I was surprised at how little maneuvering room the orca had in the tiny net pocket. I wanted to touch him; he would have to let me; he couldn't get away. Or could he? The fragile net barrier was an enigma. With little effort the orca could have broken out.

Using threatening gestures, an unfriendly-looking character motioned us away. Reluctantly I climbed back into the floatplane. Enroute to Seattle my only consoling thought was some information heard at the wharf. The Vancouver Public Aquarium had offered ten thousand dollars with a one thousand down payment, the balance due when the whales were safely in Vancouver. The offer was rejected, though an approach others might insist upon. Realistically, transporting the whales was an enormous gamble. Those other buyers could pay a high price, but were they gamblers? I would risk it, but could ill afford to lose.

Three days later, on a Saturday afternoon, I was plucked from the aquarium crowd by the public address system. "Ted Griffin, phone call."

"Are you still interested in a killer whale?" the voice sounded thousands of miles away. . . . "Are you there, Mr. Griffin?"

"Yes. Go on."

"The little whale, she got away. Do you want the big fellow?"

I quickly thought how I might raise fifty thousand dollars, a figure previously mentioned by the fishermen. No, there was only one whale now. Would they accept twenty-five thousand? No good to offer a down payment, too risky for them if the whale escaped. It was a cash crop, like the salmon. Somehow I would raise the money. I had to!

My long pause brought an anxious question, "Ah, ah, how much will you offer? As is, where is."

In the darkness of my thoughts I began to see a point of light. The other buyers had wanted the small whale. Were the three fishermen without any buyers? I dared not insult them with too small an offer. I knew how impulsive they could be.

"How much are your three nets worth?" I asked.

"Oh, the nets? Ah, new, say about one thousand apiece, and they're in real fine condition." I paused, waiting for him to digest that bit of information. He didn't argue; I continued, "Here is my best offer, all cash in advance. I will pay three thousand for the three nets, and five thousand more for the whale, a total of eight thousand, U.S. currency. When I've removed the whale you can have your nets back."

"Mister you have bought yourself a whale, but we have no more time to waste. You must be at the cannery tomorrow, Sunday, before midnight. We've already lost too much fishing time. You get here or we'll cut the whale loose!"

"It's a deal. You have my word. I will be there with the money." I continued gripping the phone in both hands, as if it were a link with the whale. *He's mine! I'm going to have a whale.* I finally replaced the receiver, wondering: *what have I done? Where will the eight thousand come from? How will I transport a four ton bull, or is he five tons?* Feeling as though my life was suspended in the balance, I planned in detail the next twenty-four hours. With no turning back, I committed myself totally to get that whale home.

"Jim, I made a deal for the Canadian whale."

"Ted, that's wonderful!"

"I must get to the cannery town by tomorrow midnight with eight thousand cash or they'll let the animal go."

"Eight thousand cash? What are you going to do for money?"

Sunday morning I stopped at each place of business along the Seattle waterfront and announced, "I bought a killer whale."

"Yeah? Really?"

"I'd like to borrow as much as you can spare. Will you accept a check you can't cash for awhile?"

The shopping bag I carried soon filled with green paper, fives and tens and twenties. I was worried about being robbed, and got a gun. The theft of the money was of minor concern; the important issue was it would mean the loss of my one chance to have a whale.

I would need help. I had rehired Homer Snow, the animal trainer, as soon as aquarium finances improved. He was my first recruit. Jim hadn't quite the appropriate experience. I decided to ask my whale-hunting competitor, Don Goldsberry, the man in a helicopter to whom I yelled, "Get away from my whales." He agreed to go to Canada when needed.

Homer and I stopped in Vancouver, B.C. to pick up an armed guard, a former Royal Canadian Mounted

Policeman. Time was growing short; I asked the pilot to shortcut over land; the reply, a firm no. His decision greatly troubled me. Someone else could be racing to buy the whale now that word of my offer was in the news.

It was nearly dusk when we reached Alert Bay. "We'll lay over here for the night, Ted."

I nearly screamed. "Impossible! We have to get there by midnight. There's no other way. They'll cut the whale loose, someone might even kill him."

"There's not enough daylight to continue. You know I'm not allowed to fly this aircraft in Canada after dark."

The pilot, Don Vickery, was feeling the squeeze. There was a rising level of tension between us, but with each minute we drew nearer my goal. We passed Port Hardy and swung north over Queen Charlotte Sound. "I'm turning back," said the pilot.

"Wait, look ahead. There's light on the horizon." I was desperate. I must keep him flying north. We had flown together many times scouting for whales. He always put the safety of his passengers ahead of other considerations, an important reason why I chose to fly with him. Now I had to keep him flying, against his better judgment. There would be no turning back, but I wanted him to reach that conclusion. "You're doing fine, Vickery. We'll make it easy."

"I don't like it, Ted."

"Well, if we're forced to land we can stay in one of these little coves for the night," though for me no such option existed.

"There's not enough protection down there. The sea is running too heavy. I could lose the aircraft."

"Yes, I see your point. The sea is a bit rough. How would you handle it if we had to put down?"

"It would be dangerous, too dangerous." Perhaps unconsciously, the pilot had begun a slow, shallow left turn.

I could go to prison for taking the action I contemplated. I steadied his hand on the wheel. He turned to look at me. I searched his eyes, testing his resolve, "You're doing fine. I know we will make it, and so do you. See, there's light enough for a safe landing. You've been there before, just three days ago. You know your way into the harbor. We are more than half way now; our destination is closer than returning to Port Hardy." I sensed the pilot's great strain.

Alone, I was holding back the press of darkness with my mind, trying to save the last glimmer of a dying light.

Descending below the treetops we were pitched into darkness, then from the factory wharf one radiant light guided us. Settling slowly, Vickery was making a long, power-on approach. I gripped my seat, rigid with tension, unaware of the pontoons touching the water.

"Ted, we've landed," Vickery dead-panned. This dry response made me realize how much pressure the pilot had been enduring, and how hair-raising the night landing had been.

Homer and my guard in the back seat hadn't made a sound. Now Homer said, "I'm glad we're down, Ted. It's amazing you've lived as long as you have."

The fellow from *National Geographic* was again there to greet us, catching the plane wing and pushing us to the dock. I plied him with questions, "How is the whale, Paul? Did I make it in time? Did anyone else come to buy?"

"Relax. The whale is fine. Willie and Bob heard a plane, and in this remote town they knew it had to be you and turned in."

"I want to see them; make sure they know I'm here with the money. Where are they tied up?"

"Come on; I'll walk you over. Everybody is talking about you coming with eight thousand cash."

I caught the alert, watchful eyes of my guard. With his powerful two-hundred-pound frame, policeman's training, and shotgun ready; he was every bit the deadly force he appeared. I shrugged my shoulders under the strain of the rucksack. It was not from the weight of printed paper, but rather the eight-thousand-pound whale.

My companion continued, "The Vancouver Aquarium people are still trying to buy the bull." Apparently something had delayed them in obtaining a consensus. Their group had met several times to vote on besting my offer.

"I'm here with the cash. What can they do now?"

"They might try to stop you somehow." Others had come to bid, but gave up when the little whale escaped. The risk in transporting the big bull seemed too great. I recognized that formidable problem and soon would face it, but an even greater challenge awaited, the whale himself.

We reached the gillnetter. I shouted, "McGarvey?"

"Yeah, come on aboard. Oh, it's you. Got the eight thousand?"

"Yes; you still have the whale?"

"That whale's not going anywhere until I say so, but he's not yours yet. Sit down."

Keeping his elbow on the galley table, McGarvey raised his right hand. "Some other people want to buy the whale. Maybe I don't know if you're the right guy to have it. Put your hand up here. If you can take me arm wrestling I'll sell you the whale."

The fisherman's hand was rough; his fingers strong. They gripped mine like a vice. The muscles in his stocky forearm bulged as he increased the pressure. Why was he challenging me? If I lost, would he really refuse to sell me the whale? It seemed like a bluff, an after-midnight game of cat and mouse. But I couldn't afford to lose. *I won't lose.*

Straining, I watched his eyes. Was he getting tired? My whole body ached. Believing he had reached his limit, I visualized the great bull orca, summoned every ounce of strength, and pressed the back of his hand to the table.

"You have more under the hood than I would have thought, Griffin. You get the whale."

A few minutes later in the cannery lobby I heard someone say, "No, they're not here. They have turned in for the night." Two men hovered near the wireless telephone conferring about an expected whale counteroffer from the Canadian fishermen's union. It was rumored they wanted to keep the whale in Canada. How ironic; before last week they were killing the whales, as competitors, and as "trophies."

I took Homer aside, "You get on the phone. Tie up the line, fiddle around; do whatever is necessary. No calls can be allowed through tonight, none from the fishermen's union, nor any other whale buyers. You get my drift?"

Homer's eyes twinkled, "Don't worry. I'll take care of it."

I had an agreement with the fishermen that I intended to complete, in spite of arm wrestles or any other interference. Quartered in the cannery bunkhouse, I couldn't unwind. Protecting the prize with every fiber of my being, I regarded all sounds in the night as potential threats.

Next morning the radio crackled as we motored to Warrior Cove. I feared some new offer might come, by boat or plane or radio. Surely the gill-netter could move faster.

Homer scurried up the side of the reef and studied the whale for some time. Randy the guard, and one of the fishermen counted the money. As if from far away I heard someone say, "It's all here, eight thousand." At long last, I had my leviathan, a killer whale never before tamed, with a bloodline twenty-five million years long.

10
Through The Door

On a one-whale race I had placed my wager, eight thousand on the nose. But unlike the track bettor, I alone controlled the outcome. I didn't want to be apart from the great whale, and believed I was the only person in the world capable of caring for him, but the solutions for many problems required my returning to Seattle. Homer advised, "You better go back. With Don Goldsberry here to help, we can take good care of your animal. We know what this whale means to you." Reluctantly, I agreed.

In Seattle, interest was growing in the killer whale caught in nets in northern Canada. A reporter asked, "How will you bring the whale to your aquarium?"

"I don't know yet. I'm working on a solution."

"You bought a live whale for eight thousand dollars and don't know how to get him home?"

"Yes, that's correct, but I *do* have a few ideas."

"What about those groups trying to keep the whale in Canada?" And, "Is it true, that you plan to swim with that killer whale?" and, "How much is all this costing you?" There seemed no end to the questions. I was tired of answering them. I had to find some money, arrange for the aquarium's management, and figure out where I would put the whale once I got him home. Considering the transport problem, I resolved to maintain an open mind. My earlier belief that no killer whale could be held in a net had proved inaccurate. Why hadn't the bull broken out of the corral to join his companions? Frequently they had touched nose to nose through the nets. I worried he would change his mind later.

I called Marineland and visited the Vancouver Aquarium to ask for suggestions on moving the whale. They each responded, "If we knew the answer to that one, we'd have bought the whale." Biologists at the U.S. Marine Mammal Laboratory advised against lifting him out of the water on a a stretcher-sling to load on a freighter or plane. They said the whale's lungs might collapse from his immense body weight. In later years it was proved they can actually breathe easier out of water where there is less pressure.

I could slip a rope around him at low tide when he was nearly stranded; perhaps lead him like the harpooned Moby Doll. How about using drugs? No, authorities had recently decided that not enough was known about the effects of drugs on marine mammals. A drydock worked for Moby Doll, but when I checked, the rental fee was astronomical, and none were available for weeks. They had said it wouldn't be safe to tow one in open water. Was there an amphibious aircraft large enough to take the whale? I had no answers . . . yet believed a solution existed.

By visualizing, I could get my subconscious mind to work on the answer. I saw him coming home, the tasks that might be involved. I felt the emotions, heard the sounds of whales and men and ships, smelled salt air, diesel exhaust, and fresh fish.

Next day eating lunch near the aquarium at Ivar's restaurant, I had the feeling that everyone stared at me, seeing a whale instead of a man. Finishing with the steamed clams which Ivar called brainfood, I removed my bib and felt an urge to sketch on the placemat. As ideas tumbled out in a rush I drew plans for transporting the whale. By mid-afternoon I was lining up supplies all over town. "Port Hardy on Vancouver Island? You bet. I can fly you out first thing in the morning."

Twenty-four hours later my supplies were lying in the grass at Port Hardy and the twin engine aircraft was a dot on the horizon. I walked to town and hired the first driver and truck I found to transport the cargo which included several tons of structural steel. We arrived at the docks just in time to catch the weekly departure of the northbound coastal freighter.

"Homer, how is he? Has he eaten?"

"Your whale's doing fine. I think he's eating, but," Homer's voice lowered, "we nearly lost him the other night."

"What happened?"

"The nets were down for several hours, about ten feet underwater. The whale could easily have got away. In fact we don't know why he didn't."

"What did you do?"

"Don and I stayed right beside him all night. Now this may sound crazy, Ted, but a couple times, when it seemed he was thinking about swimming away, we talked him out of it. You know, he just backed up a little, away from the perimeter. I've gotta tell you, that's one fine animal. I just hope you appreciate the opportunity he presents."

Homer's story blasted through me like a bolt of lightning, and even though I knew the whale was safe, it left me shaking. "Why were the nets down?"

"At low water they snagged on barnacles. When the tide came in, the corks couldn't rise. We realized the problem too late."

"OK, we'll build a stronger net with more flotation. . . The fifty-five gallon oil drums, did you find some?"

"We cleaned out a local salvage company. Had forty or so, but they're not happy. They use them over and over for raising sunken vessels, so asked a stiff price."

British Columbia Packers, owners of the cannery town, offered credit, the use of their dock, equipment, and some manpower. At each fishing boat in the harbor I asked, "Can you weld?" If someone nodded yes I hired him. Job interviews were never so brief. I told the welders to meet me on the main cannery wharf where a couple of men with forklifts were already at work clearing a large construction area.

One of the foremen said to me, "I hear you're going to weld out here. If so, it'll be in a rainstorm. I've got to hose the dock steady because of the fire danger."

I smiled at the pipe-smoking gentleman and said, "No, we don't want a real fire, do we?"

Within the hour men were spreading steel bars on the dock and welding them together. An elderly fisherman asked, "What are you building, son?"

"A floating pen for the whale. Do you think it will work?"

"That's up to the whale," he replied.

I pushed the crew, racing with a sense of urgency against an unknown deadline. When a welder stopped to eat I put on his gear and continued. "Zowee," an electrical shock jolted me, right through my wet tennis shoes. Some bystanders chuckled.

"Mr. Griffin, I think more diagonal bracing is needed in the corners. Where are your plans?"

"In here," I told him, pointing to my head. He smiled, understanding. I continued, "Add whatever you think is required."

The first wall took all day to construct. A welder suggested, "They'll go together faster if we assemble them flat on the deck and tilt them into place." I put that man in charge and offered him a bonus. Another crew welded the bottom, similar in construction to the walls.

Work continued nearly around the clock. With no

committees to consult, I could make immediate decisions, and avoid delays. Right or wrong, I alone would bear the consequences.

Homer and Don were rarely seen in town. On one of my daily visits to Warrior Cove, Don told me the new heavy duty seine net was doing the job of containing the orca. Requesting several hundred pounds of salmon, he added, "We'll just eat what the whale eats."

In four days the forty-foot by sixty-foot pen was completed. The structure, standing twenty feet high, resembled one of my many childhood Erector-set projects. Ready for launching with one end open for the net doorway, the pen had forty-one bright-orange oil drums providing flotation.

"It'll never hold that whale," said a man watching from atop a stack of fish boxes.

"I bet it won't even float. Probably go straight to the bottom."

"That is, if they ever get the contraption off the dock. Ha, ha, ha!"

My construction project amused a number of local residents. I was too tired and busy to pay any heed. At high tide I positioned a barge with an A-frame boom at one end of the wharf, and two forklifts at the other. Designed to hang suspended from the flotation drums, the pen's long steel spans collapsed like limp spaghetti between the lift points when we tried to move it. I was really stumped.

News of the comical launching effort brought many cannery workers and townfolk to watch. They gathered quietly in small clusters, oblivious to the light rain. From the sympathetic expressions I sensed some would like to help, but didn't know how.

"OK, Ted, I've got it welded back together, and we're all hooked up. Shall we try it again?"

I walked toward the fellow, then impulsively turned to the crowd. Unable to see very many faces in the late evening darkness, I focused on the small group closest to me. "I have a problem here," I said. "I would appreciate it very much if some of you would help me get the whale pen launched."

For a silent moment no one moved, then four people stepped forward. As though rehearsed, the spectators one by one took positions around the huge cage, including a few who had bet I wouldn't succeed. All told, about a hundred men and women grabbed the cold steel bars and lifted. They walked to the pier's edge carrying the pen, then released their holds at the last moment, turned aside and walked back. The orderly scene reminded me of graduating seniors receiving diplomas.

"Hey, look at that, it floats!" they cheered, and I felt a tightness in my chest. The pen worked just the way I planned, yet in the water it suddenly seemed too small. I was more anxious than before.

"You cannot keep a whale's spirit confined. We believe the orca are like gods. To injure one brings bad luck. Just you try to put him in your cage, you'll see." Some of the fishermen in the town were members of Indian tribes. They spoke to me about their belief that confining the whale could bring me harm and cause them a poor fishing harvest.

I listened, but all I could say was, "I understand how you feel." My desire to befriend the orca was at least as strong as their wish to have it released. I mentioned to Don that some fishermen were unhappy with my action, "There's talk of releasing the bull. Better prepare for trouble."

"Not all of them feel that way. We have a few on our side."

Don and I were cramped in the galley of a gill-netter. Looking at his rugged frame and bold, angular, sometimes handsome face disappearing under a fast-growing beard, I realized I hardly knew the man. I had asked him to join me for two reasons: he had sought whales on his own initiative, and his boss had told me, "You won't find a harder worker with commercial fishing experience."

During the last eight, hectic days Don and Homer had been almost constantly with the bull so I sought their counsel, "Do you think he will go in the pen? Once we get him in there how will he behave?"

"He's been nearly stranded in that rock pocket some part of each day. Just waits for high tide to float him out. He doesn't show any sign of panic," Don answered.

"A very intelligent animal," said Homer, "you move slow, let him figure out what you want, he'll cooperate."

"How do we position the nets so that he will swim through the door?" I asked.

Don was sketching left-handed while we talked. Turning the drawing toward me he answered, "Like this, through a big underwater funnel. We'll get one chance, Friday morning at low tide. The water will be slack for less than an hour. If we don't have him in by then, forget it."

The boat's owner and a partner in selling the whale looked over Don's shoulder, studying the sketch. The sparkle in his bright, alert eyes revealed he was itching to get in on the action. I asked him, "What do you think, Walter?"

"That's the way I'd do it; the way he's got it there. Only one place for that whale to go. You boys will have to be very, very good though, no mistakes. Tie up everything nice and tight; it ought to work."

The little tug, "Robert E. Lee," had chugged into harbor on schedule. Aboard were four men: my public relations consultant, Gary Boyker; Seattle radio personality Bob Hardwick, who owned the vessel; and two fellows from the *Seattle Times*. The next day Hardwick hooked up a tow line to the newly completed, steel cage and we headed toward Warrior Cove. The gasoline-powered tug struggled, the drag of the floating pen immense. Don looked worried, "The tug is really heating up. I don't think she will make it all the way to Seattle."

"Yes, I agree. We'll have to think of something else."

"What did *National Geographic* say?" I asked.

"They want your whale story. A partial payment arrived today," Paul said. The news and money were most welcome, though the major financing for the venture would have to be figured out later. Getting the whale home was so important to me that I operated on a no-limit budget. My full attention had to remain focused on that elusive "door"—the philosophical door of opportunity—linking me with the whale. Don had said it would open briefly the next morning, then close with a slam, perhaps forever.

In Warrior Cove a light mist drifted up from the calm water. I faced the rising sun, eyes closed, and felt its radiant energy flowing through me. The sounds were soft, distant: heightened voices, engine noises, whoosh-oop. A stocky man worked, directing the crew, setting heavy anchors, securing lines, darting from boat to boat with speed and agility. The gaze of several fishermen followed his movements, then turned to one another registering approval of Don's expertise.

Homer called, "He's curious, Ted. Look, probably wondering what we're up to. Hey, Ted!"

"Uh? Oh, Homer, what?"

"The whale, he's watching us. I'll bet he knows."

"We're all set," said Don; "it's time to lace her up."

The floating pen was anchored in place with its open end, the door, against the whale's nets. I shrugged off drowsiness, slipped into the cold water, and found relief from the wetsuit heat buildup. Visibility was poor, unlike other days, less than a foot in the murky brown ocean. I started lacing the whale's net to the pen, working by feel, sewing with nylon seine twine on a fisherman's needle. I put on an Aqua-Lung to complete the forty-foot bottom stretch. EEEE—URRH—EH, EEEE—URRH—EH, the high-pitched sound seemed to reach me from all directions. A chill moved along my spine; *hurry up, hurry up,* my inner voice urged. Out of twine, I surfaced.

"Here's your cord, but watch out," Homer's voice was anxious. "That whale is acting just like a cat, watching every move. Hovers right over you; maybe he likes your bubbles."

"Tell him I would taste awful. Toss him a salmon."

Was the whale's curiosity a prelude? Homer said he was a cat, maybe I was the mouse. I felt the pull of tidal current. It had started sooner than we planned. Not much more to go, but I had to hang on to prevent being swept away. EEEE—URRH—EH, EEE—URRH—EH. I decided to humor him, "Eeee—urrh—eh." I was amused at my presumptuous little squeak. Continuing lacing, I tried again louder, "eeee—urrh—eh."

"EEEE—URRH—EH!" The response was immediate. Wonder what I said? What he said? "EEEE—URRH—EH, EEEE—URRH—EH." He sure was a talker. Our little exchange intrigued me.

"Eeee—urrh—eh."

"EEEE—URRH—EH."

I waited, unwilling to move, holding fast to the net; the silence, the darkness, unnerving. Then I called out again, "Feee—urrh."

"EEEE—URRH."

Something inside me stirred, tears came to my eyes, scenes from the past flickered before me. Although many others feared the whale's attention, I inexplicably derived pleasure from it. Happy, excited, I shivered with anticipation, then felt my way to the next mesh, passed the needle through, around the steel bar, and cinched it tight. "Eeee—urrh—eh."

"EEEE—URRH—EH."

Rising to the surface I shouted, "All laced up."

Don was anxious, "Get moving. We're behind schedule. Cut the nets; get the door open now."

Swimming inside the pen I sliced my way to the bottom, taut cords parting like butter with the touch of a razor-sharp blade. When the opening was almost complete, I felt a sudden chill, then ropes and nets fell on me. They had started too soon! *Must have thought I was clear.* They were sinking the corkline with heavy weights. *I'll drown!* The strong current tugged at the nets, ensnaring me. I struggled but the tank held firm. Clamping my teeth on the mouthpiece, I slowly wriggled out of the air-tank harness. By slashing the nets I finally worked my way free. I worried there were more nets overhead. I couldn't see at all. *Have to chance it.* I swam upward; it was all right, no more nets. Breaking the surface I saw the killer whale only a few feet away. Such a huge mammal; I stared; he stared. I hoped Gary Keffler was right, that whales weren't interested in divers. I wondered if this orca knew that. Little use to escape death in the nets, only to be gobbled by the whale. The bull seemed curious, but came no closer. I lingered, feeling euphoric.

"Ted, hurry it up! We're losing too much time." Don's sharp voice conveyed his concerned state of mind.

"I was all tangled down there. My tank..."

Don interrupted, "Never mind; get out. We've gotta move fast now." Rowing a small dinghy behind the whale, he dropped a lightweight seine net in a semi-circle. The big orca swung around to inspect the new fence. Not liking the change in accommodations, he furiously blew bubbles and squeaked in protest. "Easy, boys, easy now; we don't want to push him." Standing in the dinghy, Don directed the two teams placed on opposite corners of the pen who were drawing in the circle of net. This was the most dangerous time, for men and whale.

The bull maneuvered with remarkable agility in the ever-smaller enclosure, turning upside down. His fluke brushed the flimsy net, almost jerking it from the men's hands. The orca neared the pen's forty-foot-wide door; plenty of room, but he was resisting. "Don't get tangled, whale." I feared he would smash through everything. The drum inside me announced every passing second. "Keep going, that's the right direction, yes, yes."

"Stop pulling; let HIM make the choice," Don called from his precarious position in the little boat, only a few feet from the frustrated whale. Like tracking radar, all eyes focused on the creature. Pounding his pectoral flippers and swinging his tail in protest, the whale submerged.

I held my breath. Compressed within each moment was the fear of tragedy, the hope for success, and a vision reaching to the end of my life. "Please, whale, find your way."

Grim faces broke into uncontrollable joy. The watercraft rooting section raised a cheer, ringing the ship's bells, blowing their whistles and horns. It was a celebration of victory, and more, a salute to the whale, who for now had acquiesced, and entered into a human world. Quietly,

in sober reflection, Don, Homer, and I closed the "door."

A strong tide pulled relentlessly at the pen anchored in Warrior Cove. Tightly drawn fibers almost twanged as I cut the nets, releasing the pen. The tow began, then Don shouted to Hardwick at the tug controls, "Hold up!" The towline slackened; everyone watched for the mammal. When the whale surfaced facing the rear of the pen, Don shrugged and said, "The tide is putting us on the rocks. We can't wait until he turns around. Have to chance it." He spun his finger in the air, signaling to start the tow again. The pen headed north, the whale facing south. I clenched my teeth, but the orca suddenly performed a slick little somersault, surfaced belly up, and swam the proper direction with effortless grace.

A wild jungle animal would surely test the strength of its confinement, but the whale kept clear of the steel mesh walls. Perhaps all those days confined in Warrior Cove accustomed him to a restricted environment. He rolled to one side, holding his head just above water, and watched his watchers, most of the two miles to the cannery town.

11
Journey

Two hours later we completed the tow from Warrior Cove. With news of the whale's arrival at the little community where I had built the pen, people streamed out of the cannery buildings onto the wharf. A native boy leaned over the side of the pier, calling to the whale, "Namu, Namu, please hear me, Namu," his voice clear, filled with optimism.

"That's it!" I said. Homer had suggested I name the whale after this town in British Columbia, but I had been undecided. I didn't know the word's meaning, only that it was the town's name. Hearing the boy call, I thought it sounded just right. I told the gathering, "I will name the whale Namu, in appreciation for the help and cooperation so many of you have shown."

Nearly everyone wanted to shake my hand and offer good wishes. An Eskimo said, "No harm can come to you by this whale. Embodied within him is the spirit of man."

A woman cannery worker cautioned, "The responsibility for the life of this whale is in your hands."

I'm sure they wondered whether I understood the whale's significance in their culture. The mystique of the orca was symbolized in Indian totem art and popular in local legends. One man offered me a roll of sailcloth. I hesitated, then unfurled the canvas, and found a painting of a mythical killer whale. "Is this your work?" I asked.

He nodded. I was deeply moved by this gesture from Stephen Hunt of Bella Bella, British Columbia, all the more important when some others objected to my taking the whale.

A fisherman slapped me on the shoulder. "You won't hold him long. When the big fellow makes up his mind to go, he'll walk right out of your contraption."

"Maybe, but I'm betting he won't."

"More like praying, I'd say." His remarks brought a hearty laugh from friends, and even a small chuckle from me.

Since Hardwick's tug couldn't manage the long tow to Seattle, Don and I asked among the fishing boat captains at the wharf. One agreed to take the cage as far as Port Hardy.

Walter, one of the three fisherman who sold me the whale, asked, "I'd like to make a few improvements to the whale cage. OK?" His narrowed eyes showed concern.

I answered, "Sure, but the skipper wants to get underway as soon as possible."

He and several recruits lashed long fir logs under each row of drums. Two boom logs were positioned, forming a triangle in front of the pen. "He won't get away now, Mr. Whaleman. The big logs in front will break the wave action when you're in the rough stuff."

"I should have thought to do that myself, Walter. I really appreciate everything you have done."

His eyes were wide and bright, his smile reassuring. "Just get our friend home safely. That will make it all worthwhile." With pride he handed over the towline, the same rope I had brought along the day I purchased the whale. I smiled inside, remembering how I had planned to loop it around the orca's tail and lead him back to Seattle.

As the journey began, the frantic pace of the past two weeks slowed. Namu swam with ease, seemingly unaffected by his vastly restricted environment. Passing Warrior Cove I found it strangely silent. Abandoned strings of white corkline swirled aimlessly in the tide, giving little indication of what events had transpired earlier that day.

Breaking through a wall of tension, a flood of aches nagged at me. After buying the whale I had labored under relentless pressure. Inexplicably, the greater the problems and corresponding stress, the higher my level of intoxicating energy. My focus on one objective, the whale, activated a remarkable physiological and psychological mechanism preventing collapse. Without recognizing it I had run a gauntlet of sorts. Walking into an airplane wing three days ago had given me a jagged cut over one eye, slow to heal. A leg infection, origin unknown, grew larger and more painful by the hour. I wanted only to sleep and sleep.

One day out of the cannery town our expedition cleared the southern end of Calvert Island; losing our protective landfall, we were vulnerable to the full force of the Pacific Ocean. In Queen Charlotte Sound, eight to ten foot high rollers swept past, lifting the pen, arching it across each wave's back, then twisting steel bars the opposite direction in following troughs. The doomsayers had warned, "You'll never make it. That contraption will break apart in the open sea." And it nearly did, but the crossing to Port Hardy would take only two days. Namu seemed to enjoy being lifted up and down on the rollers.

Life aboard the little tug settled into a routine: Bob Hardwick made morning broadcasts to his Seattle audience on the ship-to-shore radio; Stan Patty and Bruce McKim, the *Seattle Times'* feature writer and photographer, were fast becoming involved in the success of the journey. Gil Hewlett, a staff biologist with the aquarium in Vancouver, British Columbia, was a last minute but welcome addition to the crew. Had his aquarium's offer for the whale been accepted, I would have been *his* guest. Gil sat alongside Namu, recording his vocalizations and noting the corresponding behavior. Namu's utterances, when played back, had a lyrical, almost hypnotic quality about them. Hour by hour the whale drew us closer to him. Our thoughts concerned little else.

A minke whale coming in from the ocean swam toward Namu. I had thought other sea mammals were afraid of killer whales. Passing within several yards, neither showed an interest in the other. I saw no sign of the friendly whales from around Warrior Cove. I was told Namu had moved in and out of the net the day of his capture. The fisherman had thought Namu was trying to lead the smaller whale to freedom through an opening. When the nets shifted during a tide change, both whales became trapped. Several days later the little one escaped, joining the cow and calf which had remained near their netted companions. The so-called vicious predators' capacity to care for one another gave me much to think about.

A single-engine float plane circled over Namu's pen, then with flaps extended, settled slowly into the ocean swells. As the Cessna 180 taxied toward our tug, I recognized the passenger, Emmett Watson, and felt a twinge of uncertainty. Columnist for the *Seattle P.I.*, Emmet was the major competitor for Stan and Bruce, representing the *Times* and already traveling on the tug.

Sitting across from Emmett in the little tug's semi-private cabin, I thought the newspaperman's deep-set eyes bored holes in the surroundings. We began the interview discussing little things. Emmett was smiling and I felt relaxed; he was surprisingly easy to talk with.

"Namu has caused quite a stir in the Northwest; people want to know more about you and your whale. What kind of man wants a killer whale for a friend?"

Someone who never wanted to grow up, I thought. Instead I answered him, "I recall the first time I saw a whale up close. I imagined I could befriend it. You know, Emmet, the sea has always been a magnet for me, but something was missing. I was lonely. I wanted an animal companion completely at home in the ocean."

"I think others have felt the same, Ted, but what made you decide on a killer whale?"

"They're intelligent, Emmet, and a little bit scary. There's something about all that strength and ferocity. I wanted an animal friend which could protect me. A killer whale could. That quality increases my risk, but I'm excited by the challenge, attracted by the danger."

"When did you sleep last? You look as if you have nearly killed yourself getting this whale."

"Yeah, Emmett, almost." I remembered how I had nearly drowned in the nets at Warrior Cove the day before.

"What are your plans now? Will you swim with Namu? Will you ride him?"

I thought, *swim with the whale? Yes, but ride him?* "Well, one day, when the time is right, when we become better acquainted."

I felt a rapport with the newspaperman. When he asked permission to accompany the whale on the remainder of the journey, I was torn. For a while I couldn't resolve the pull of loyalties. I wanted to say yes but the tug seemed too small, so many possibilities for friction. Reluctantly I refused him.

The afternoon of the second day we reached our first stop on the north end of Vancouver Island. Almost the entire population of Port Hardy, B.C. was on the wharf to greet us. The skipper and crew of our tow vessel, eager to be on the fishing grounds, took a last look at the whale, wished me luck, and were gone. When they faded from the horizon I felt stranded.

The whale crew were instant celebrities, but we had little time for the limelight. Don and I slipped into the cold water to survey the pen and found considerable structural damage. Fatigued and broken steel supports were

Bella Bella

NAMU
Warrior Cove

Calvert Island

Rivers Inlet

Queen Charlotte Sound

Johnstone Strait

BRITISH COLUMBIA

Port Hardy

Alert Bay

Kelsey Bay

Seymour Narrows

Campbell River

Powell River

Comox

VANCOUVER

Georgia Strait

VANCOUVER

Port Alberni

Nanaimo

Tofino

ISLAND

Gulf Islands

San Juan Islands

Bellingham

Deception Pass

CANADA
U.S.

Sidney

Victoria

Strait of Juan DeFuca

Whidbey Island

PACIFIC OCEAN

Port Angeles

Everett

OLYMPIC PENINSULA

Bainbridge Island

SEATTLE

Vashon Island

N

TACOMA

SCALE IN MILES 0   50

NAMU'S JOURNEY ················

WASHINGTON

replaced and welded; chain and rope had to suffice for underwater repairs. The pen had just barely survived its first crucial test.

Namu watched us work. He reminded me of my two-year-old son, Jay, following me around the house, curious about everything I did. In the remarkably clear water the entire whale was visible for the first time. I felt dwarfed; the whale below water was enormous, almost as big as a locomotive. He was much thicker through the neck and chest than I had imagined. With great dexterity he used his front, pectoral flippers to maneuver in a variety of ways.

Jim was relieved when I phoned the news of our safe arrival in Port Hardy. Proudly he said, "I got Lloyds of London to write whale life insurance. All risks are covered except escape. The waterfront merchants are so excited with the prospect of a killer whale attraction in Seattle that they increased their cash guarantees, even your landlord is in on the deal."

I was reminded of the Dutch boy who plugged the hole in the dike; Jim certainly had plugged the holes in my finances. My nature was to take incredible risks if the potential reward was great enough, sometimes even venturing beyond the point of no return. Not so with Jim. He'd get just as excited as anyone about a new undertaking; then he had the remarkable ability to step back and take a hard look. If he decided the deal was OK, my brother would go for it, but hedge his bet and place a limit on his exposure.

Annoying rumors floated about town. I became wary when hearing the Canadian fishermen's union had not given up. "They're going to stop you from exporting 'their' whale, legally, or otherwise," I was told.

The *P.I.* reporter, Emmett Watson, had surprised me by asking, "What will you do if someone tries to set the whale free?" I had thought it was a ridiculous possibility, but in Port Hardy I learned that a Seattle private detective had been hired to do just that. The controversy dramatized by the press had inspired animal protection societies to demand, with religious zeal, the whale's release. I queried a friend, "What is this free-the-whale movement? No one ever gave a darn about the killer whale until last week. They hated them and shot them. Now all of a sudden people are beginning to think of them as human."

"I think you mean, more important than humans, don't you?"

"More important?"

"Sure, isn't that the way people react, emotionally, to sub-human creatures?"

"I don't understand. More important? What sort of stories have been in the press?"

"Don't worry; you can read them when you get back to Seattle. Your job now is taking care of Namu."

"What if someone tries to cut him loose?"

"That could be a problem."

Stranded in Port Hardy, plagued with rumors of an attempt to release the whale, working night and day to prepare for the next leg of the journey, I had become exhausted. I cheered when the sixty-five-foot vessel that Jim had arranged for finally pulled alongside the whale's pen. In a brief conversation with the skipper of the Seattle-based tug, "Iver Foss," I found him long familiar with log towing, winds, and tides. He was well suited for the task and had all the answers, except the one I wanted most, "How long will it take?"

He responded, "We'll just have to see how it goes. There is no telling. The tug's owner, Mr. Foss himself, told me to take no chances with this one-in-a-million whale."

The elite crew of our small tug returned from town loaded with food and supplies. Don saw me gazing into the distance and walked over, pressed his hand on my shoulder, and turned me to face him squarely. "You look tired, in fact, hang-dog tired. Fly home; rest for a few days."

"No! I can't leave Namu."

"Who says so? Sure you can. Nothing is going to happen to your friend. I'll look after things for a few days. Namu will get more care than any whale in history."

Reluctantly I agreed. A float plane about to leave for Seattle had room for one more. Gaining altitude in the aircraft, I spotted movement in the water several miles away and turned to the pilot, "Look at that herd of killer whales. They're making flank speed directly for Namu." Watching helplessly from the air I agonized with the thought of Namu trying to join them. "Don, Don, are you on the radio?"

"OK, Ted, take it easy. I see them."

"What's Namu doing?"

"Thrashing around a bit."

"Trying to escape?"

"Not yet."

Reaching the pen the frisky whales frolicked about the surface. They were so congested I could have walked across their backs and kept my socks dry.

"Hey, Ted, everything is OK. It's Namu's buddies from Warrior Cove. They're settling down; go home."

In Seattle I got a medical check-up, antibiotics for the leg infection, and rest. The reporters waiting at the aquarium had more current information about Namu than I. They didn't believe me when I couldn't tell them exactly where the whale was. I escaped and rushed to buy some newspapers. Stan Patty wrote in the *Times* a blow-by-blow account of the whale's progress with colorful, personal profiles on the crew. I got so caught up I almost forgot my own involvement. Stan speculated on what the mammal might be thinking, on the whale's personality. Though he tried to maintain an objective style of reporting, his growing fondness for the whale showed through.

Day by day a confrontation was growing between the city's two powerhouse daily newspapers. With the *Times* reporter practically sitting on the whale's back, the *P.I.* was left out, scratching for the essence of a story they might rather have ignored. The *Times'* ability to keep Namu in the headlines forced the *P.I.'s* participation. I was told the *P.I.* reporter, Emmet Watson, depicted his counterpart as "the Brand X reporter who could not track an elephant in a snow storm with a nose bleed." Stan wisely ignored the remark, keeping his energy focused on the whale story. With surprising insight the *P.I.* found other dimensions of the episode; the coverage was often humorous and perceptive:

> Ted Griffin, the energetic, resourceful and sometimes short-fused owner of Namu, your friendly and personalized whale, appears to have succumbed to the duties of greatness.

I laughed at myself, for they saw some truths I had missed. Namu was swiftly capturing the hearts of an emotionally receptive public.

Returning to the expedition, I stepped out of the float plane and was immediately aware of a change in attitude. "We didn't expect to see you," they said. During my brief trip to Seattle the group had pulled together. For the duration they considered the whale "theirs." I felt like an outsider.

On board the little escort tug, living conditions were extremely tight, requiring each crew member to have unusual tolerance for their sleeping companions and someone else's salty clothing. The whale's magnetism cast a spell over the diverse individuals. Somehow it all worked. Loyal to the task of getting Namu safely home, they had all vowed not to shave until we reached Seattle, at a time when virtually no one had a beard. The crew members, with their counterparts one thousand feet away on the larger tug, were immersed in an adventure, when people said so few were left in the modern world.

Don Goldsberry had assumed full responsibility. He enjoyed the environment and the challenge, primarily a physical one requiring great strength and stamina. The two *Times* newspapermen had proved surprisingly capable in their dual roles, carrying a full share of the work. Creative, multi-faceted, and a fine seafarer, Bob Hardwick, the tug owner, kept the crew on balance. I could not fully assess Namu's significance for him. Perhaps he shared some of my aspirations to become acquainted with the whale. Our Canadian observer kept to himself, not allowing all the hoopla to muddy his objective, probing mind. He was looking forward to the day when Vancouver would have another killer whale like Moby Doll. Little did I suspect at that time I would later capture the first whale displayed at their aquarium in Stanley Park. They would keep Skana for thirteen years.

A cow and two calves followed our flotilla. During quiet moments they came alongside Namu. "The same ones from Warrior Cove," Don insisted. The unwelcome arrival of a lone bull upset Namu when it appeared the bull was trying to run off with Namu's entourage. I named the interloper "Oil Can Harry." Whenever Harry came near,

Namu thrashed wildly, tossing his curved flukes high in the air, then pounding them on the water. Remarkably the caged whale kept clear of the steel bars and inflicted little damage to himself, but finally Bob Hardwick took action. Maneuvering the tug near the intruder whale, he dropped several weighted firecrackers over the side, and drove the character away.

The captain of the large tug had more to think about than whale domestic problems. He studied the tide tables and listened to weather reports, carefully selecting a time to run the treacherous Seymour Narrows. Erratic currents and shallow reefs have sunk so many ships there, it is called the Maritime Graveyard. At four a.m. the Foss tug inched out of the secure little cove, whale pen close-hauled for better control, and our tug behind. We were quickly caught in the tide, running like a river, with no turning back, no place to stop. The swirling water buffeted Namu, who had to maneuver constantly to keep from being tossed against the steel walls. Then our ordeal quickly ended. Hardwick summed up the two hour passage best, "Seymour Narrows has some of the most turbulent water in the northern hemisphere, but for us it was Lake Placid."

I flew back to Seattle and a few days later got a message, "It's Don on the phone."

With barely a hello I asked, "How is Namu?"

"He had a sunburn, but I was able to cover his fin with a quart of zinc oxide. He's better now. We've got to hold up; the pen is breaking apart. Can you send some help?"

"Sure, Don, right away." I chartered a plane and loaded it with repair equipment, then phoned my longtime friend at Underwater Sports, "Keffler, Don is stuck in Comox Harbor; the whale cage is breaking up. He needs a diver. Can you help?"

"Sure, I'll go. How do I get there?"

"I'll fly you up, sitting on a barrel of chain."

"Just so we're not too heavy for take-off. And I want the scenic route coming home." The damage was soon repaired and the traveling whale sent on his way.

Sixteen days out of Namu Cannery I rejoined the group for the border crossing, relieved, believing I was free from possible Canadian entanglements. We quickly cleared U.S. Customs and Immigration at Friday Harbor, though the taxable status of the whale was in question. They considered calling him livestock, even whale meat. Government agents had been debating the imposition of a duty, though the Washington State senior senator, Warren Magnuson, had previously stated none would be assessed. My contention that Namu was a U.S. citizen returning from a summer vacation in Canada didn't carry any weight with the bureaucrats.

Winding our way down through the San Juan archipelago, we passed a little tug in the channel. Though the tide was against us both, the tug was struggling to hold its own. In a kind of tow-yoke similar to my own, the "overtaxed" vessel was hard at work dragging along thousands of logs. I was reminded of the ever-present problem, the revenue collectors seeking yet another way to extract taxes. Later they levied a sales tax against the whale.

I received notice from the Washington State Department of Fisheries that it was illegal to feed the whale any fish suitable for human consumption. We had been buying salmon along the way from fishermen. The State Highway Patrol was advised to make an arrest if I violated the law. *The highway patrol?*

While planes circled overhead, dozens of boats followed the celebrity. Like a veteran entertainer Namu performed barrel rolls and somersaults, then popped his head up to look at the audience. Boom, boom, Namu slammed his giant pectoral fin flat on the water's surface. He was agile and alert, though a little thinner since his capture. A

slight depression had appeared behind his blowhole. I wasn't sure how much of his daily rations he was eating, if any.

Returning to the aquarium, I prepared for Namu's arrival in Seattle. Local residents waited to welcome their new "citizen." Fifty miles to the north, automobile traffic was stalled for hours. *Seattle Times* photographer Bruce McKim captured the dramatic moment. I still remember that scene, thousands of curious, excited onlookers were jamed along the rails of the Deception Pass bridge, watching the whale pass one hundred fifty feet below.

During those eighteen days in July of 1965, Namu traveled four hundred miles. Finally he was in local waters. I had thought the journey would last little more than a week. Filled with anxiety and a little frightened of my growing fame, I could stand on the pier and see the flotilla just across Elliot Bay, but Namu was not home yet. I would have to wait until morning.

12
Whale Town

Weren't you taking a big gamble, Mr. Griffin?" a reporter asked at an interview in front of the aquarium, "betting sixty thousand dollars you could bring that whale to Seattle? A lot of people thought it was impossible."

"Yes, it was risky, but feeling the way I do about killer whales, I just looked at the problem differently."

"It is cruel keeping that whale in a cage, just to make a buck," an onlooker announced.

"Some people feel it is cruel to confine any animal, especially whales," I responded, "but I disagree with them. Whales are not human; though at times I've wished they were. Animals have become acclimated to restricted environments, zoos and the like, for thousands of years. That's how man has been able to study and learn about them. Public display of Namu may earn a few bucks, but it is the only way I know to pay his maintenance expenses. The money as an end in itself could never have motivated me to such extremes. I have risked everything, including my life, on the strength of an idea; believing it is possible to make friends with a wild killer whale."

"If you plan to swim with the whale, what precautions will you take?"

"I don't know. How could anyone rescue me if he attacked?"

"We hear he eats a lot of salmon. What else have you learned about Namu?"

"Well, who would have thought an orca could have such strong family ties? Namu even tried to rescue a young whale when they were first trapped together in the nets. On the other hand, it is well known orca kill sea mammals. Some believe they kill humans. However, working in Warrior Cove a few feet from the killer whale, I was not attacked. We even 'talked' to one another, you might say. I think people's fear of them stems from ignorance. I intend to show orca are not dangerous to humans, and can be tamed. I hope people will change their attitudes about these whales and stop killing them wantonly."

High thin clouds diffused the orange ball of early morning sunlight. Its brightness seemed to emanate from all directions. The warm air was still, almost a hush, reflecting the mood of the expectant crowd gathering on the aquarium pier. One mile across placid Elliot Bay the collection of pleasure craft and commercial boats turned toward Seattle, accompanying the killer whale on the final stretch of his long journey. Aircraft circled in the cerulean blue sky. Unable to bear the suspense, I took Pegasus across the bay to be with Namu. When the whale's pen neared the aquarium, the large tug, Iver Foss, released the tow, handing the line over to the escort tug, Robert E. Lee. While the band played a rousing melody, Hardwick's jubilant crew eased Namu's pen into the mooring area at Pier 56. The cheering and applause grew louder; the celebrity whale, as if on cue, performed a series of roll-overs, and demonstrated upside-down swimming, with a tail-lobbing finale. A flood of tears blurred my eyes. "This is the greatest moment of my life," I said, choked with emotion, and found it nearly impossible to speak any more to the assembled dignitaries. I was sad; the saga was ended. Then I felt lifted with thoughts of the one soon to begin.

Losing myself in the duties of entrepreneur, I added another ticket seller and shifted barricades to prevent any more free viewing. For three years my business had operated on the edge of failure and I had reluctantly considered closing after the summer season. The whale could be my salvation. I wanted to bring people into my underwater world, have them discover the breath-taking beauty and solace of undersea life, so different from the terrestrial one. I wanted the exhibits to entertain, excite, and challenge the viewers; to say, "There's more here than meets the eye."

Throughout the aquarium I heard people talking about Namu. Excitement ran high. Though a few carried signs, such as "Free the whale," many were ecstatic with the opportunity to see a killer whale. A number of people have genuine empathy for animals, particularly dolphins, and are concerned with their welfare. I understood how they might have felt, the orca seemed too large an animal to keep in a small cage, but it was a temporary measure. I had plans for a big oceanarium with a whale lagoon.

Stepping into the quiet office, I could still hear the roar of background noise, the public address system, fragments of conversations. Inspecting the "key to the city," I remembered someone saying, "A gallant man and a magnificent feat." I felt embarrassed. After all, so many had played a part. I hadn't done everything. Yet any "magnificent feat" begins in one imagination. I realized that in pursuing my goal I had touched many other lives, launching some on a course parallel to mine, whether they sought adventure, knowledge, money or whatever else.

As thoughts tumbled about, I experienced a let-down and strolled out to Namu's pen, inching my way through the visitors for a place at the rail. The whale surfaced. Rolling quickly on his side caused his dorsal fin to slap the water loudly; he flipped his tail as he dove. I hoped it was a greeting to me.

A week after Namu's arrival, we manhandled the whale's pen out of its mooring and secured it alongside the Harbor Tour float. A dozen skin divers moved to key locations around the cage, with exact instructions. Having no way to anticipate the whale's behavior when we inserted the liner under him, I reiterated, "If he shows any signs of distress, stop everything!"

The Herculite Company had learned of my concern that Namu had to swim in the polluted water of Elliot Bay. They offered eight thousand square feet of their highly-durable coated nylon fabric. The Seattle representative had worked night and day to assemble the material, delivering it in just one week.

We began the dangerous task, drawing the eight-hundred-pound liner slowly across the inside bottom of the pen. Namu exhibited erratic behavior, then "parked" underwater in the far corner, his blowhole submerged. Everyone stood watching the whale. I feared he would go berserk, breaking out of his pen, fragile from the sea voyage.

"What's he doing now?" I shouted to a surfacing diver.

"Watching me," was the casual reply. I prodded Namu with a pole; he remained motionless. I didn't know how long he could stay submerged without drowning. I wanted the divers to push the whale, but realized that could be dangerous. When ten minutes had elapsed I decided to try pushing him myself. As I entered the water, the whale stirred. Slowly, deliberately, Namu inched himself out of the cramped corner. I couldn't tell if he was in trouble. Finally he rose, and took a measured breath. The divers quickly went into action, pulling on the lines that brought the fabric across the bottom, while the whale was at the surface. Within minutes all was secure as planned.

"Well, Keffler, what do you think?"

"I think we were darn lucky, probably just pawns in the whale's game of chess."

At the rate of a thousand gallons per minute, clean water poured in. By late afternoon I could see all of Namu, even the bottom of his new pool. The whale certainly was friskier, and now I could check for uneaten fish. Although others disagreed, I believed Namu had eaten very little, if at all, since capture.

A sturdy rowing skiff, needed for maintenance, was tied inside the pen. Namu's curiosity was aroused. When he nudged the boat with his chin, it bounced around like a piece of driftwood.

Killer whales, like dolphins, are thought to enjoy rubbing one another, but Namu had no companion. He appeared to be scratching his head on the little skiff's bottom. I attached a broom to a long pole and pushed it toward him. He kept his distance. I persisted; eventually he allowed me to touch him with the bristles. I brushed him until he moved away. Soon he was back for more. When the broom was held firmly, he undulated his back against it.

At last, I felt a direct link with the whale; in a way, Namu was responding. Though I couldn't get him to take fish, as Moby Doll had, he would readily come to be broomed.

A few days later my brother came with friends to visit the whale. "How's your appetite, Namu?" Jim asked. He removed his suit coat, rolled up his shirt sleeves, and descended the ladder. "Come on, Namu, this is fresh caught, not that old junk Ted is trying to feed you. If it's not fit for human consumption, why would you want it?" Jim casually splashed the fish, much the same as I had with Moby Doll, then held it beneath the surface. Namu swam toward him and, without hesitation, took the salmon.

I ran over, "That's the first time I've actually seen Namu swallow a fish. Do you have any more?" Jim offered the expectant animal a second, firm, fresh fish. Down it went. "I'm glad you got him to eat, but you just broke the law. Are you on good terms with the highway patrol? Maybe we could get Namu reclassified."

Jim responded, "There are a lot of people out there who seem to think he is human."

Soon after, a special short-term exemption was made in Namu's case, allowing him to eat whatever he liked.

After Jim's visit, one meal usually consisted of several hundred pounds of fish. Oddly, tuna, codfish, and herring were rejected; he accepted only the most expensive, salmon. By what process did he discriminate between various fish held under water? He didn't tear them apart, or even inspect them, just refused to come to the food station.

A woman traveled across the country and told me she had felt compelled to visit Namu, saying, "There is no explaining my feeling. It was as if the whale had called me."

She wanted to touch the orca. "Sure, come on," I responded, "let's feed him."

After offering Namu several ten-pound salmon which were quickly gulped down, the woman said, "You don't know what a thrill this is for me. Come here, big fellow; let me scratch your chin."

Others came, some from as far away as Europe, expressing a similar mystical calling.

While I was lunching with friends at "Ivar's Acres of Clams," the owner came to our table. "Take good care of our whaleman here," he said to a surprised waitress.

"Hello, Ivar. What do you recommend today?"

"Why, Ted, you know everything we offer is excellent. By the way, is there going to be a shortage of salmon this year?"

"Oh, you mean Namu; you never can tell; better stock up just in case."

"OK, keep clam, Ted."

When the delicious seafood arrived, I mentioned to the guests how Ivar, Lynn Campbell the Harbor Tour operator, Chuck Peterson of Trident Imports, and others along the waterfront came to my rescue with some of the funds to pay for bringing Namu to Seattle.

Namu was on his side, motionless, looking up at me. I knelt in the bottom of the little craft, peering over the rail at the whale. The scene was reminiscent of my early encounter with a whale at Richmond Beach. With a playful nudge, the four-ton orca nearly dumped me. I touched his skin with the brush. He gave a little start, but didn't move away. Working with the long handle, I scrubbed his back. Great clouds of sloughing skin and algae washed away. He rolled upside down; I worked on his belly. He raised one pectoral flipper to be brushed, then the other. I reached with both hands and started rubbing him gently. My hand movements were like the strokes of a blindman exploring the size and shape of a companion. His skin felt sleek and very firm. The slightest touch of a finger registered a response. The spectators were unusually silent, almost transfixed.

When I climbed up from the pen, many aquarium visitors encircled me: "Unbelievable. How did the whale get you started scrubbing him?" And, "Can you do that any time you wish?"

And, "Do you know Ted Griffin, the whaleman?"

"Sometimes," I answered with a quick grin, "but like his whale he is difficult to get to know."

"What kind of person is he really? The stories are mostly about the whale."

Later I introduced myself.

"Oh, ahh, I thought you would be much older. Why did you do it? I mean, a whale?"

"I wanted him for a companion, like a dog or horse. I grew up around water, swimming every day, diving with makeshift equipment before skin diving had become a popular sport. I wanted an animal to accompany me in the ocean, and an intelligent whale seemed a likely candidate. I am fascinated with the challenge. For some it is a climb up a mountain, for me it is winning over a very wild and dangerous creature."

"Your friend, Lynn Campbell, is calling on the ship-to-shore from his Harbor Tour boat. He says there is a large pod of killer whales racing into the bay."

I ran outside with field glasses. Namu was shrieking and lob-tailing; he knew they were coming. From several miles away I saw them heading directly for him.

In a minute Pete was at my side, "Hey, what's with Namu? I could hear him shrieking from the back of the aquarium."

"Look out there, Pete."

"Do you think Namu will try to escape and join those whales?"

"He didn't in Port Hardy, but cross your fingers."

About three hundred yards away the visiting whales suddenly stopped. Some of the pod leaped high into the air. Back and forth they swam, up to an imaginary line, but would come no closer. Great streams of bubbles burst from Namu's blowhole, his voice a shrill pitch. Then as quickly as they had come, the pod of whales turned and rushed out of the bay.

Namu pushed the little boat with such exuberance that I stretched neoprene skin diver-suit material over the skiff's bottom to protect his beautiful skin. Every hour I rowed around the enclosure to entertain visitors. When I suspended a fish over the water, Namu opened his cavernous mouth. Looking at his two big half-circles of thumb-sized teeth, I wondered again about swimming with him. I had been playing with the whale for about three weeks, protected by the boat. Believing he had a gentle nature, I nevertheless feared what might happen if I entered his pool. Quite possibly he would turn on me. Whenever I left Namu, he appeared to sulk. Sometimes he would slam his tail, splashing water everywhere. That could be a sign of ill temper, or an expression of fondness for me. He gave no cause to fear harm, yet I remained apprehensive.

At each day's end I would tally the aquarium receipts. It was often long after midnight before I had the task completed. Unfamiliar with sorting and counting such large sums, I found the stacks of paper bills inevitably tipped over and fell to the always-wet floor. Somehow I never tired of picking them up. I soon paid back the eight thousand I had borrowed from the merchants that Sunday morning. It looked as though Namu would earn the rest of the sixty-thousand-dollar trip. I tried to relax a little, but couldn't; my inner spring was always tightly wound.

Recognizing the need for some help at the aquarium, I thought of just the man and called Tacoma. "Don?" I asked.

"Hello, Ted. How are things in the big city? Is Namu packing them in?" Goldsberry's voice was heightened.

"The whale is just great, eating lots of salmon, but around here it's a madhouse. How about yourself? What are you doing since you got back from the expedition?"

"Same old job, though now I'm considered the resident whale expert. I've been asked to talk about the Namu trip, and have been giving a number of slide shows. What's this I read in the Seattle papers about Namu eating salmon while poor people go hungry?" he asked.

"You know what skillful newspaper reporting can do to stir up controversy. But they don't say who is going to pay the fishermen to catch salmon. Namu at least earns his keep."

I finally got around to the point of the call, "I'm all bogged down, can't find enough time to enjoy Namu. I could use a man like you at the aquarium. Will you think about it?"

"I like the idea. Let me call you in a few days."

Don accepted my offer. It wasn't long before we were talking killer whales. One day I asked him, "Would you help me capture an orca, a mate for Namu?"

A broad grin preceded his answer, "When do we start?"

13
Orcology 101

The well-publicized accounts of the capture of a killer whale, and his unusual journey to Seattle, piqued world-wide interest. I received many long-distance calls: "Is your whale still alive? living in the cage? There's been no news coverage here for several days." And, "I'm traveling to the west coast on business. I would like to stop by and meet Namu."

There were a number of callers seeking scientific information. One was a private contractor conducting dolphin studies for the Office of Naval Research. Another came from the Scripps Institute.

The first call came from the Boeing Airplane Company. Curious about Namu's squeaks, wails, and clicks, they sent a research vessel to record his vocalizations along some of the journey to Seattle. Preliminary investigations revealed most sounds were made when the whale released air past the muscular flap over his blowhole, although sometimes he uttered similar sounds with no corresponding release of air bubbles. The frequencies, mostly from one thousand to ten thousand cycles per second, were within the human audible range. Though it appeared the sounds were a form of communication, they were also thought to enable navigation. The scientists wanted to know the effective range and accuracy of the whale's sonar.

In discussions with Ted Walker from Scripps Institute, James Fitzgerald doing research for the Navy, and others who came in 1965, I inquired about the killer whale's potential for training, for learned behavior, and for work. I was told their brain is one of the largest among the whales, roughly equal to that of a blue whale, whose body is many times larger. Generally, scientists believe the size of the brain, in relation to an animal's body weight, is an indication of its intelligence. The orca brain, though four times larger than a human one, has to control a body nearly one hundred times larger.

Since the killer whale is a giant relative of the dolphin, much of the early dolphin studies, including their sonar ability, should hold true for orca. The tursiops dolphins have demonstrated competence in a variety of assignments, including working underwater with humans. Dolphins can differentiate very similar objects, even within fractions of an inch. Can a whale be trained to "tell" what it has "seen" with sonar?

I had thought there would be some military interest in the whale's abilities, but in 1962 the U.S. Government publications had stated the killer whale would attack and kill any human in the water, even though there were no confirmed human deaths by killer whales. I hoped that if Namu's behavior convinced the military, and others, to alter prior misconceptions, then the prevailing attitude would change for the better. After a Navy admiral went swimming with Namu in his pen, the U.S. military became interested in killer whales. I was asked to visit the Pentagon that year, 1965, to discuss my findings and theories with the Navy's department of anti-submarine warfare. Three years later in 1968, the U.S. Navy purchased two killer whales from me. They were taken to Makapuu Point near Honolulu, Hawaii for study and training.

I felt the orca had potential for transporting people and equipment long distances. The whale's body shape helps it slip through the water at high speeds with very little resistance. It may be a coincidence, but the nose of a Boeing 747, viewed head-on, is amazingly like the shape of the first third of an adult male orca.

I speculated that the whale might prove useful in one form of ocean ranching. Fish such as salmon, tuna, and other schooling varieties could be driven into mid-ocean holding traps. There are logistical and feeding problems for such large creatures, of course; but I think killer whales can be trained for this work and be allowed to live free in the ocean. Extending the strong attachments exhibited for one another to their human contact will be an essential part of such a program. Like a horse plowing a field, the whales could perform services: search and rescue, coastal guard duty, carry a modified TV camera for underwater inspection, and other possibilities.

Dr. Thomas C. Poulter, director of biological sonar research at Stanford Research Institute, made several trips from California during 1965 and 1966. This interesting man was second in command on Admiral Byrd's expedition to the South Pole in 1933-1934 and directed the scientific research. He saved Byrd's life at the Pole by removing him from an instrument "blind" full of carbon monoxide. In Seattle one day he said, "Ted, I'd like you to listen to these tape recordings. The first one was made when you got the whale several months ago." I was mimicking the sounds made by Namu underwater.

"And now," Dr. Poulter said, "the second recording was made this morning."

"Tom, I'm getting to sound more like Namu. Do you think some day I'll talk like a killer whale?"

"Perhaps." His face expressed slight disappointment, then an understanding smile. "But that's not what interests me. Namu is the one getting better. He has changed, apparently trying to match your sounds. Your talk is unaltered."

"The whale has taken the initiative?"

"Sounds that way."

Dr. Poulter later transcribed the recorded vocalizations into printed graphs called sonograms. His early studies enabled him to identify individual animals by "voice print." It appeared there might be several messages superimposed on the basic tonal frequency. Deciphering the whale's "language" would be a long and difficult task. Tom said then, "The energy level of the killer whale's call, much stronger than a common dolphin's, should enable orca to contact other whales miles away. When the orca sounds are played back through high quality underwater speakers to other marine mammals the results might prove interesting."

Dr. Merrill Spencer, director of the Virginia Mason Research Center in Seattle, wanted to learn the secret of the whale's breath-holding ability, believing the medical benefits for man could be significant. I put up a small amount of cash enabling Dr. Spencer to begin a pilot study on orca. Leaning over the side of the small boat, I attached a suction-cupped electrode to Namu; the first electrocardiogram of a free-swimming orca was obtained. Dr. Spencer said, "This is great stuff. At the start of the whale's dive his heart rate is about seventy beats per minute, like ours, but look what happens toward the end. The heart rate drops roughly in half. This is how Namu conserves the oxygen in his blood."

Other studies during 1965–1966 indicated the cardiovascular system of cetaceans reduces blood flow to non-essential extremities when necessary. The marine mammals' capability for redirecting blood/oxygen to the brain and heart is now called the "diving response." As compared with humans, the marine mammal is believed capable of utilizing three to four times as much oxygen from each breath of air. When all these factors are combined: reduced heart rate, redirected blood flow, and greater utilization of oxygen, it becomes clear how the whales can remain submerged for such long periods of time.

14
Courtship

A light breeze swept clean the morning air. Sparkles of sunlight danced across Elliott Bay, converging on Namu. A large crowd stood in line waiting to see the killer whale. My brother appeared, escorting two men along the public walkway overlooking the whale. I greeted them, "Hello, Jim, Ivan, Lamar."

"Good morning, Ted, how's Namu today?"

"Fine. Why don't you go down and visit him?"

Ivan Tors, producer of the popular TV series, "Flipper," and his cinematographer, Lamar Boren, descended the ladder to the whale pen. When they were out of earshot, Jim said, "They went for it, Ted! We have a deal to make a feature motion picture. They want to start right away, filming in a natural setting. I told them you want to exhibit the whale at the aquarium until the end of the summer tourist season. Oh, one more thing, they insist you swim with the killer whale. They have to show it to the film's backers; otherwise, it's no deal."

"Sure, Jim," I gulped, not ready to go in with Namu, "maybe in a few weeks."

He shrugged and walked away. Just over a month had passed since Namu arrived in Seattle, yet I didn't feel secure with him. I had been enjoying new celebrity status: the press conferences, the speaking engagements, contracting for Namu records and souvenirs, talking with the children who recognized me from frequent TV appearances. Public life had consumed me; at times I felt a stranger to myself. My original purpose in obtaining a

123

whale was getting pushed aside. For the first time I experienced some uncertainty.

The movie people returned up the ladder. "Namu is wonderful. Will he come when you call?"

"He knows the sound of the dinner bell, but I'm not sure he knows me yet."

"Is the visibility always like this? I couldn't film underwater in these conditions."

"This is typical of Elliott Bay. Five to ten miles away it's better."

I was surprised to see Jim sitting inside the pen dressed in a wet suit, dangling his feet in the water. Namu showed little interest, so my brother slipped in with the orca. What the devil was Jim doing? Namu circled the pen, eyeing him.

"Hey, Ted, you sure this is a *killer* whale?" Jim hollered.

Darn, my brother was baiting me. I was unprepared but had to make a move. When I joined him in the pool corner he climbed out without a word, the smirk on his face remarkably revealing. I approached Namu with the usual long-handled brush. He allowed me to scrub him, taking no particular notice that I was in the water instead of the boat, I saw a few anxious faces among the people watching from the pier, mostly unaware that this was my first time.

Easing my hand over his nose, I was able to stroke him gently. I moved closer, reaching higher. He moved forward, pushing me with his snout, pushing hard. He could crush me against the pen! Just short of the bars, he stopped. On the second attempt, he was more forceful in driving me away. I was very disappointed.

Lamar descended the ladder dressed in a black wet suit. A man of ample proportions, he looked to me somewhat like a whale. Underwater with his huge camera positioned like a shield, the cinematographer motioned me toward the animal. I swam around Namu in wide circles, finally approaching with brush extended. This time the whale was more accepting, allowing the familiar grooming. I released the brush and cautiously touched his body with both hands. As my fingers moved down his spine, he arched his back like a cat; he enjoyed the stroking. With increased courage I submerged under the orca. He tilted on his side, watching me out of one brown eye. With almost imperceptible contact, my hands traveled over his body. I experienced a strong sense of *deja vu*, of having previously been in the water alongside a whale. My vision at Richmond Beach had come true; it was just as I had imagined it would be.

Surfacing, I reached for his dorsal; the tall fin trembled as my fingers gripped tightly over the edge. Namu jumped forward, pulling free of my grasp. When I tried to regain contact, the mammal circled, always out of reach. Then Namu slowed; with a reckless lunge I grabbed his fin again. Instantly the orca surged ahead, dragging me. Mask and snorkle were stripped away. From the shock of cold water blasting through my wet suit, and momentary blindness, I let go. Feeling rejected, and afraid that he was about to turn on me, I considered giving up.

Diving to the bottom I easily recovered the shiny face mask; recovering my self-confidence was another matter. In the westerns the wild pony throws the cowboy and he must get back on the horse immediately or the animal will never be ridden. Having sustained no injury, I gathered the courage to try again. Approaching the "horse" took patience. Holding my mask in place, I grabbed his dorsal fin; Namu bolted! Teeth clenched, I hung on with all my strength. The water pressure built, tearing like a hurricane, pounding my body. The orca

dropped his head and raised his back high above water. I spiraled forward; bucked off again.

I felt exhilarated, but in rushing an undefined time-table, I had taken liberties and invaded Namu's space. Someday I would ride him. Recovering my equilibrium, I swam to Lamar's corner and saw the excited look in his eyes. "You sure have your hands full with that whale. Great footage. How about keeping Namu occupied while I climb out?"

"Sure, Lamar."

United Artists agreed to back the whale film. They would pay twenty-five thousand dollars for the rights, all whale maintenance expenses, and hire me as technical advisor. If they knew how hesitant I had been to go in the water, and what reservations I still had, they might not have been so quick to make a deal. For several days Lamar and I searched for a quiet, clear-water lagoon suitable for filming. We found Rich Cove near Bremerton had plenty of tide action to keep the water clean.

I had the problem of transporting the whale again. Underwater inspection of his pen showed it had nearly disintegrated, the nylon-reinforced-Herculon liner was all that prevented escape. Don and I scrounged around in junk yards until we located just the thing, a Navy surplus anti-torpedo net constructed of heavy, interconnected cable rings. With large cedar logs for flotation, we fabricated a new, smaller, travel pen. Towed by one of Lynn Campbell's Harbor Tour boats, Namu again crossed Puget Sound, though this time almost unnoticed.

When we arrived at the cove Namu wouldn't leave his pen. He floated, facing out toward the channel. He had exhibited this behavior from the very first in Warrior Cove when he generally faced the deepest water. We had started that first tow with him facing backwards because the tide was putting us on the rocks. When leaving each port along the journey he had faced the channel or any visiting whales until the tow began, then quickly adapted to the direction of travel.

We tried using a net to get Namu into Rich Cove, but he wouldn't budge. Keffler, myself, and several other divers entered the water. We formed a wall around the whale and began shoving him to the rear of the pen.

"How can we tell if he is going to attack?" a new recruit asked.

"After he eats you," I retorted. "Keep pushing." When we got him turned around, he swam under the log and through the open net gate.

Namu darted away, conducting a tour. He inspected the patch of sun-bleached oyster shells brought in to improve visibility for filming, then followed the more-than-two-hundred-foot-long dock to shore, and swam back to us at the perimeter net. The tip of the orca's fin cut a thin wake at the surface, a large wave forming over his rocketing body, then he leaped!

I was filled with happiness watching him, sensing he liked his new, very much larger quarters. I wanted Namu to be free, yet couldn't part with him then. I had to fulfill my dream of interacting with a killer whale. If Namu was tamed, I would make my home on Puget Sound. The great orca could come and go as he wished. Until that time I would have to live with the contradiction.

The narrow country road leading to Rich Cove filled with vehicles and curious folk. I engaged a security guard and a deputy sheriff to control the crush of spectators.

The firmness of the wet suit felt good, propping me up, easing the hollow nervousness I had experienced all morning on this first day of filming. With the rising tide, bits of dry wood and seaweed floated about my feet like so many little islands. The sun broke through the clouds;

soon I was roasting in a black rubber stew pot. Would Lamar ever finish his blasted light meter readings? Namu cruised back and forth just offshore, watching our every move.

"Ted! I want you to enter the water from the shore." At last, relief in the icy-cold bay. "Now get the whale's attention. Don't look at the camera. We're not interested in your good looks." When I was waist deep, Lamar called, "Hold it there. OK, now call the whale."

Bending over with face in the water, I began, "Eeee, urrh, eh, eeee-urrh-eh."

"That's it. He's on his way; good, keep him coming."

"Eeee, urrh, eh."

"A little closer, come on, whale, just a little closer." The tone of Lamar's voice conveyed his mounting excitement.

Namu swam toward the beach. I felt great apprehension. Again the whale held the power of life or death for me. Standing chest deep in water, facing the huge beast, I tried not to be frightened. The behemoth approached, looming before me. I wanted to run, get out of there. He had been exceptionally rambunctious that day. Thoughts of his killing ability were driving me wild. It was too late for retreat—Namu had almost reached me.

Ten feet away the big mammal ran aground. Bouncing his belly on the sandy bottom he couldn't easily come any closer. He arched his back which raised his tail and head. Suddenly I felt the whale wanted me to come.

"Go to him," Lamar shouted. "Easy, go slow, act like you're just getting acquainted; that's it, now explore him a little."

I spoke to the whale in my thoughts, *We are friends, you and I, we have much to accomplish together*. My anxiety abated. I felt a warmth within me as a barrier fell away. Moving to Namu's side, I patted him cautiously. He pushed toward me, nudging against my legs, rubbing slowly. A large wave settled him closer to the beach, white underside pressing on the sand, bulging his belly. I walked out, rubbing along his side. Namu turned his head to watch.

"Can you climb on his back?" coached Lamar with great delight. A small crowd of spectators had somehow inched their way past the guard. In contrast with the camera team, their faces showed grave apprehension.

"Now don't get nervous, whale." With both hands I reached overhead for the dorsal fin. "Easy, fellow, that's it, let me hold on." Inch by inch I raised one knee after the other, crawling up his side.

"EEE, EEE, EEE."

"Not yet." I swung one leg across the animal's broad back and sat astride the killer whale; this was no dream.

For a moment Namu remained still. Then, with a gentle, rocking-chair motion, he undulated his tail. I grasped the fin firmly, expecting the whale to dislodge me. The orca belly-bumped along the bottom like a blubbery harbor seal humping its way over land. Foot by foot he reversed off the beach. *I must escape before we reach deep water, jump!* I thought, but the burning desire to ride an orca kept me seated.

Without submerging, the killer whale turned and swam to the center of the lagoon. "Hang on, Ted, ride him, cowboy!" Lamar shouted. Namu carried me to the corkline, along the rocky shore, then back toward the beach. Our speed increased; I gripped tighter, pressing my shoulder to his dorsal fin. *No, Namu, don't dive; I can't*—The pounding water blasted me from the whale's back.

Where was he? I opened my eyes; he was swimming straight at me like a run-away freight train. Instinctively I tucked into a tight ball, protection against being rammed. He swooped past, brushing so close I bounced and spun along his side. When I looked again the whale was beside

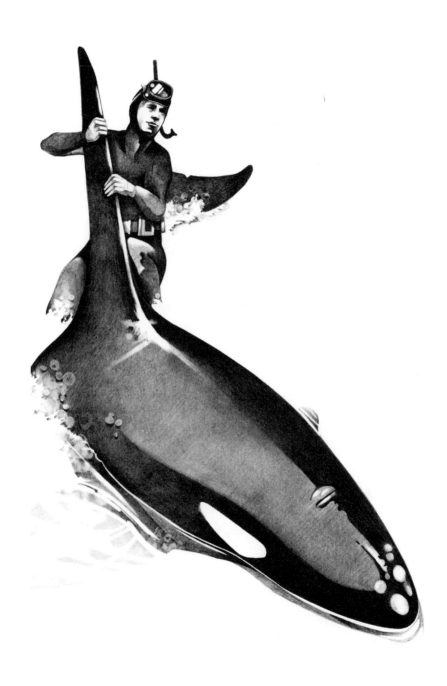

me. I waited. He waited. I moved slowly, grasping his dorsal fin—instantly he darted off. Unable to remount my swiftly-moving steed, I was unceremoniously dragged along. Near shore I let go. My knees nearly buckled as I walked out of the water. Lamar was beaming, "Ted, you did it! You're the first person to ride a killer whale. This is a memorable day."

I hadn't yet realized the significance of the occasion, then wondered if Namu would ever allow me to do it again. I was so overwhelmed by the event that I didn't hear people talk, or have any awareness of my surroundings, for a while.

Driving home later, a plan came to mind. I wanted to build a really big facility for Namu. I was sure thousands, even millions, would enjoy watching the big fellow cavort with people. Aboard the ferry I remained in my car, not wanting others to intrude on my thoughts.

The film producer phoned from Culver City, California, "I've just viewed the footage Lamar sent down. Great going! I envy you. Perhaps someday you'll let me swim with Namu." Ivan Tors' affinity for animals came through in his voice. When he arrived at Rich Cove a few days later, he was like a kid with a new pet, adopting the whale feed station as an informal office.

"Is Namu eating well? Is he happy?" he asked me the first day.

"I'm doing everything I can, Ivan. He eats all he wants. Happy? Perhaps that's just a human experience we apply to animals."

"Is the whale ever aggressive toward humans?"

"No, not yet, but maybe Namu is unique among orca."

"Wouldn't it be ironic if all killer whales are friendly like this one? Most of the information about their nasty behavior would be obsolete."

Ivan left two days later. I long remember his parting words, "Take care of that whale. There may be no others like him."

Thin persistent rain settled silently on the surface of Namu's lagoon, woven into intricate designs by the gusting wind. The faltering, dark-grey light had robbed any chance of filming. Lamar and his crew took the day off. The tip of Namu's dorsal fin cut through the water at high speed. When he turned sharply and stopped, his tail popped up. He was keeping himself amused I guessed. I was happy for that. One of my concerns was that Namu might become bored so I began to think up ways to keep him busy.

Catching sight of me, he ambled over. I offered a salmon; Namu didn't open his mouth. That wasn't like him. I talked through the two-way, underwater speaker, "Come on, whale, stop the horsing around. Open up."

"EEE, EEE, EEE." No air bubbles were released with the sound. Waving a fish, I ran down the dock; Namu lunged after me. Near shore he stopped, but the wave he made crashed on the beach.

"Here, take it." He tilted his head up slightly, under the out-stretched salmon. His mouth opened a little, a little more, then I saw. A foot-long starry flounder was swimming inside a fence of yellowish teeth. The flat fish looked uninjured, even a little passive. "Hold it right there." I reached in and easily grasped the fish's sandpaper-like skin, jerking it from the captor's mouth.

"EEEEEEE," Namu shrieked at me and bobbed his head. I dropped in a salmon; slurp, it disappeared, but

Namu wasn't satisfied. "EEEEEE – EE – EE – EE," *give it back*, he said.

"OK, OK, don't snap at me like a hungry dog." Cautiously I slipped the flounder back into the whale's jaws. Namu pulled away. The bottom-dwelling fish swam out; escape was brief. "Namu, you play like a cat." He managed to eat several more salmon without losing his captive. Like a hunting dog, he cradled a living thing in his jaws without injury, and with no training. The whale could be so incredibly gentle.

On sunny days the crew filmed Namu swimming left, swimming right, swimming upside down, and from every angle in the lagoon. On especially bright days Lamar worked underwater. As the filming progressed with the actors at Friday Harbor, they sent requests for specific action takes. I generally doubled for the male lead in scenes with the whale. Ever since that first time in the cove, Namu had readily accepted me as a rider.

I was becoming complacent about Namu's ability to injure me. I began thinking of the one-sided result of a hostile encounter. What would it take to make him angry, to cause him to turn on me? I decided to test him before mealtime.

Namu's jaws swung open, tongue quivering at the sight of salmon. Deftly substituting one of my swim fins, I dropped it in. The mighty jaws remained wide apart. A slight turn of his head allowed the fin to float out. "Well, what about a chunk of rubber wet suit?" He was not interested. A block of wood? Politely refused. Clothing soaked in salmon blood? He clutched a loose corner of the sweat-shirt in his teeth and bobbed his head; a morsel of salmon spilled out and was eaten.

"Namu, you look hungry." He shook his head, then chased along as I ran, porpoising excitedly. Dropping prone to the walkway I remained very still for several minutes. Crawling to the edge, I peeked over. Inches away one brown eye stared at my blue eyes. "Not giving up, are you?" I slipped a salmon part way into his waiting maw, and yanked it away. "Come on, go for it; last chance." Though I tried several times, his broad pink tongue arching high and twitching, the bear-trap jaw could not be tricked into closing on a disappearing fish. He didn't even seem annoyed.

Kneeling, I reached into his mouth past the interlocking teeth, and grasped his football-sized tongue. In the other hand I held a four-by-four fence post ready to block his jaw open, just in case. "Why don't you do something? Think I'm your dentist?" He was very polite and never moved. Exchanging the block of wood for a salmon, I stuffed it into his mouth, holding on tightly. That did the trick; he clamped down.

"STOP! Namu, don't!" His teeth held my upper arm; he was dragging me off the float. When I resisted, he released me with the fish still in my hand. I repeated the action, but he would not close on my arm again.

Was Namu's delicate sensitivity natural to all killer whales? I found so many similarities between this giant dolphin and other pets, such as dogs and horses, that I believed the orca could be domesticated.

The rain continued. Accustomed to California sunshine, the film crew were put off by our Northwest weather. At first disappointed at the pause in filming, I soon came to treasure the solitude at Rich Cove, and the opportunity for more encounters with Namu.

One eye out of the water, the tuxedo-clad *maître d'* escorted me back and forth the length of the dock. On that cold morning I had already worked up a sweat setting Namu's table with the four-hundred-pound daily ration of fish. He paddled over upside down, using his pectoral flippers like oars. Plunk, the salmon dropped into the cavernous mouth. Swinging his head in a smooth, deliberate motion, the whale ejected the fish. "Why, Namu, what's the matter?" Each successive offering was refused. If he didn't eat this batch, I would have to sell thousands of pounds of frozen salmon at a loss.

The dark-colored carcasses, obtained at a low price from a state hatchery, were quite soft from the rigors of spawning. Namu, accustomed to the bright, fresh, firm, King salmon, was expressing himself very succinctly.

"Namu, are you bluffing?" With exaggerated movements I turned my back and moved the food can away. Was he watching? If I peeked, he would have called *my* bluff. I walked briskly toward shore, the whale in pursuit. Avoiding eye contact, I got just a glimpse of his head swinging from side to side. In the shallows he veered away, pounding his giant tail. With the follow-through of a practiced golfer, I completed my swing, continuing inside the cottage out of Namu's sight.

After a suitable waiting period, which coincided with my patience wearing out, I returned to the feed station. I offered the whale a fish with its nose cut off; the hatchery had recovered a small, coded implant to study salmon migrations. Slurp, he ate the unsightly fish; as many, and as fast as I could offer them. Turning my back and walking away had conveyed my firm refusal to offer any other food. I think he understood. I was greatly relieved. Two problems had been solved. Not only did he eat less expensive fish, but the state had permanently exempted Namu from the non-human provision of the fisheries law. The hatchery personnel had laughed when they learned of the decision, "Does that mean Namu has become a human, or have we been reclassified as whales?"

Feeling a little wild and carefree, I impulsively jumped in the water behind Namu with a salmon in hand. The killer whale lunged for me. It was too late for retreat. Underwater, I reached out with the fish. His large pectoral fins swung out like French doors, halting his forward motion. The fish was slurped right out of my hand.

I stood on the dock at day's end with arms folded and stared at the bewildering creature; he had deeply touched me. I felt a sense of longing, and a blossoming affection.

Namu didn't resist when I placed a hand over his blowhole. Several minutes elapsed; he remained nearly motionless. I changed hands, sliding one over the other. More minutes passed; I grew concerned; he was so still. Unable to hold out any longer, I shifted my hand to one side; Namu blew. Instantly I returned my hand, preventing inhalation. He settled deeper until his blowhole was below water. I felt his body surging gently with the undulation of his flukes. Nearly sick with nervousness, I was compelled to pull my hand away. In an instant Namu popped his blowhole above water and inspired, breathing several times in rapid succession. Again, whoossh, but before he could close the cover on his five-inch-wide air hole, I poked in my index finger. The muscular flap squeezed tightly shut.

"Oouch!" Pounding on his back didn't cause him to release me. I was trapped. What if he submerged? Finally after a minute he blew again, blasting me full in the face, releasing my finger undamaged.

I felt excited, but torn between the emotional strain of trying the experiment and concern for his well being—and mine.

Namu swam out of reach, taking several unemcumbered breaths, and a leisurely saunter around the lagoon. Why hadn't he displayed aggression, or distress? I had exhibited both toward him. I was struggling to understand and punishing myself in the effort. So far I was the victimizer and the victim. I stood on the dock and yelled, "WHO ARE YOU ANYWAY?!"

"EEEE, URRH, EH," *ah, come on,* he was saying. Enticingly I sashayed a salmon across his chin while treading water, then whisked it behind my back when he tried to take it. Slowly Namu circled, I turned with him, always keeping the food just out of reach. "EEEE, URRH, EH," his call sounded like a demand. I nearly handed over the fish to relieve my anxiety.

"Don't get careless, big fellow." I had withheld the food longer than usual. He brushed his nose across my belly; it felt like sandpaper across my raw nerves. I wanted to get outside my skin. He pressed forward, pinning me against his snout, moving me swiftly away from the safety of the dock. With a swing of his head he sent me spinning, and politely confiscated the source of his frustration, the salmon. I had no clue to his temperament; he had no facial expression. Inches away he waited.

Regaining my composure I grasped his dorsal, swinging easily onto his back. He lifted his spine high, tail above water. With a powerful thrust we were headed straight for the feed station. Because I enjoyed the attention I received from teasing, and was still testing his patience, I jumped clear of his back and stroked the other direction towards the shore. Without slowing he turned, dipped his head, and swept me up solidly on his back. Seconds later we were again parked alongside the barrels of fish. He reminded me of a "barn-sour" horse who always wants to turn home for the feed bucket. I would have to change the routine, maybe feed Namu intermittently from different locations around the cove.

I wished we could go on a long ride, out of Rich Cove, north past Everett, maybe through the San Juan Islands to visit the film crew at Friday Harbor.

Finishing breakfast, Namu settled himself across the lagoon, unlike his usual habit of waiting for me to swim with him. I called; he didn't respond. Had I finally made him angry? My self-confidence faltered. Perhaps he no longer found me a suitable companion. Having no enemies, his gentleness could stem from a lack of fear rather than devotion to me. If Namu only wanted a little time for himself, then my anguish was for naught. Our lives had become so entwined that any thought of estrangement, no matter how slight, struck my psyche with great impact.

15
Answering The Challenge

Say, Mr. Griffin," the night watchman said, "Namu's been kinda restless lately, slapping his tail and shrieking a lot. Other whales made so much commotion in the channel last night, slapping their flippers on the water, that several neighbors woke up. They called and complained."

"Sounds like Namu's friends paid him a visit, Tom. Did you see any whales?"

"Well, this morning I was really concerned because I thought I saw Namu outside the log boom. I figured he was gone for sure. When he came up to breathe next to the float, that was a worry off my mind."

"Very interesting. One of these days I'll go looking for those visitors. Maybe we can find a companion for Namu."

The cinematographer grinned from ear to ear, "Ted, it's definite; Ivan wants to exercise his option to film a whale capture. The movie producers authorized the expenditure of twenty thousand dollars for the effort. Can you catch one this fall before the weather turns nasty?"

"I don't know, Lamar. I'll do my best. Don and I will get started right away. The challenge of capturing a wild orca still has a powerful hold on me."

Though previously wanting Namu all to myself, even thinking *I* could substitute for orca companions, I had later decided Namu should have a mate. I left Rich Cove a little early that day eager to tell the news.

Arriving at the aquarium I located Don. "It's the opportunity we've been waiting for. Ivan Tors will pay the expenses of capturing a mate for Namu."

"Great, you know I'm ready to go," Don responded.

"All we need is a seiner with its net. Who would have thought a killer whale could be contained with one. It took the accidental capture of Namu to wake me up."

"No argument there, Ted, though in the past when orca were inside a purse-seiner's net, they always swam out, or broke through the webbing."

"I know; it's hard to figure. What's the difference between the little pocket where Namu got caught and a seiner's net?"

"That has me stumped. Let's say Namu was caught at high tide within a big enclosure. Now the tide goes out slowly. That way he doesn't panic, and the whale always has room to maneuver. I'd bet you could catch orca in a seine net and hold them, so long as they had lots of 'elbow' room. It's when you purse up and put the rings on deck, when the net pocket gets too small, that they break free."

"Somehow we'll have to keep the net open."

"OK, the seine hangs twenty fathoms. We'll take out the purse line and set in shallow water where the rings will reach the bottom. With big anchors tied to the cork-line, holding it in place, the whales will have a swimming circle six hundred feet across."

"Yes, I think they would stay in an area that size. How are we going to get the whales to hold still while we put a net around them? We'll have to know exactly where they are underwater, Don."

"That's where you come in. Use that harpoon rifle the Marine Mammal Lab loaned you and get a marker float on the pod bull. Then we'll wait until he joins the cows and they enter the shallow water. It will be very difficult, but we'll have some chance. Without the marker to follow, probably none."

A few weeks later I received a phone call. "That's right, Mr. Griffin," a whale spotter reported in October of 1965, "at least five or six whales. They're passing in front of my house now. Oh, it's so exciting to see them right along the shore."

I turned to Don in the aquarium office, "Come on, let's go flying."

We landed on the water near Blake Island south of Bainbridge. Vessels passing nearby detoured toward us to offer assistance; sea planes weren't often seen drifting in the middle of Puget Sound. The mariners were delighted to learn of the whales' expected approach and roared off to find the mammals.

"Here we go." Don spoke with a glow in his voice. "Let's see what we've got: one pod bull, several immature bulls. There goes a couple of nice-looking cows. With the calves they make fifteen, maybe twenty animals. Let's go for them!"

"You're on, Don! And look, they're going right into Clovis Passage. That's the way, just keep heading south, fellows."

A few minutes later Don shouted, "Hey, there's the Chinook. I know the skipper."

Landing, we taxied to the black and white, sixty-five-foot purse seiner. The vessel's three-hundred-fathom net was stretched from stern to shore. A tall, handsome, large-framed man, outfitted in red plaid jacket and dark wool trousers, stood with his rubber boot propped on the rail. Adam Ross, skipper of the Chinook based in Gig Harbor, had known Don for years; both as a friend and professionally in commercial fishing. "Hey, Ad," Don called out, "you want to come catch whales with us?"

"Hello, Don. You boys think you know how, eh? Where are they?"

"Coming down the pike; be gobbling up your salmon any time now. Oh, this is Ted Griffin. You ever hear of him?" Don asked with a grin.

"Yeah, something, somewhere." Adam scratched his ear.

"You doing any good fishing?" Don asked.

"Oh, yeah, some, a few, you know."

"Want to come along with us? We'll pay whatever you figure your catch would be for the day."

"Well, thanks, but I think I'll stay here awhile. See how it goes."

"OK. If you change your mind give us a call on 2182."

We flew south, landing ahead of the orca. The water was too deep and too swift to catch them in the channel. It would take them the rest of the day to swim into the lower Sound; we followed.

Near dusk I was surprised to see the Chinook heading our way. Pulling alongside, Adam called, "OK if I tag along?"

"Sure, Ad," Don answered, "but it's too late for a capture attempt today. With luck the whales are on their way through the Narrows. South of there is the only area we have much chance for catching them. Maybe we'll get an opportunity tomorrow."

When Lamar got word that we were following a pod, he collected his filming crew and equipment and joined us. During the next five days, Don and I set up base in Gig Harbor. Hiring several high school kids with speed boats, we sent them looking for whales. Each night one of the crew joined me in Pegasus. Under the Narrows Bridge we kept one another awake listening and watching for the orca which appeared to remain in the lower Sound. Each morning Don flew in the Cessna searching the four hundred square miles of islands, bays and inlets that are south of the Narrows.

Apparently the whales had split up, making them harder to spot from the air. During the week we located several stray orca but no bulls. We needed to mark a pod bull. Lamar didn't care about the distinction and rushed after them with cameras rolling. Finally at week's end, Don radioed to me, "Not much—one big cow in the Narrows."

In a helicopter I followed the animal racing north, under the bridge, surfacing to breathe precisely every fifteen seconds. "Thirty knots, maybe more." The pilot pointed to the air speed indicator just rising off the peg, and continued, "I've never seen an orca moving so fast; when she dives that whale is not out of sight for more than one or two seconds." The stroke of her powerful flukes made whirlpools visible for nearly a minute. We easily followed the animal's straight-line course. She must have known we were right behind, chasing her. She led us on and on, hopefully to the rest of her pod.

Nearly an hour later Don called over the CB, "Hey, Ted, where are you?"

"Heading for Ollala. I'm on a whale."

"What are you doing way up there? You're miles away from the pod; they're all across from Point Defiance."

Again a decoy had led me away from her pod. When I joined Don and the other vessels, the whales had crossed to Vashon Island.

"Let's try to herd them into Quartermaster Harbor. If they swim inside, we can set Adam's net across the entrance."

"It's worth a try; nothing else has worked," Don answered.

Crewmembers dropped underwater firecrackers, used by fishermen to scare seals away from the nets. The whales ran from the noisemakers. Lamar was filming from one of the speed boats as it tried to herd the orca. Off-balance holding the large camera, Lamar nearly fell out when the boat hit a big wave. Using every subterfuge we could devise, our attempt to drive the whales into Quartermaster Harbor failed. They marched straight for the harbor's entrance again and again, but each time stopped at the twenty fathom mark, turned around, and raced back out.

"Look at the chart, Don. If you're a whale using sonar, that harbor entrance would appear as a vertical wall. It rises from twenty-five fathoms to three or four. When they get inside that canyon they can't 'see' their way over the top."

We returned to Gig Harbor where I avoided the questioning eyes of the crew who hadn't been with us. "How is the filming going, Lamar?" I asked, to shift the focus.

"We have a lot of great action takes with you in the helicopter, swooping down over a whale, speed boats chasing around; but it's nearly worthless footage unless you capture one of those animals."

"The killer whales are very, very resourceful, Lamar. Can't herd them, won't go in shallow water; I've hardly seen more than two in a bunch all week, and where is the bull? Any one seen him?" None had. Without the bull, the orca never seemed to form a group.

With forehead conked on the galley table, I fell asleep haunted with whale dreams, then woke to footsteps. Adam came down the companionway looking very eager and quite serious. He called out, "Hey! You boys still interested in catching whales?"

He had been bitten by the whale bug. I saw it all in his eyes, and asked, "What have you got, Adam?"

"Some neighbors of mine called over from Wolochet Bay. They saw a few of your friends heading under the Fox Island bridge. You fellows look awfully tired. Maybe the whales are too much for you."

An hour later the cold morning air surged through the open chopper doorway. Even so, the pilot had

to rouse me from time to time. I put my face out for a refreshing blast of wind, aaaaagggh. The whales scattered, sensing the vibration of our aircraft. "They're going to be tough today. They've got your number," the pilot said.

"Yeah," I responded, "but I'm counting on you to keep me one up on them. Right?" Bob Rice smiled, then shifted his gaze to the water below.

We searched for an hour, but failed to locate the bull. A large cow came into view. Bob began a rapid descent, estimating where and when she would show again. I made the decision to try. We hovered fifty feet above the water. The big orca surfaced directly under me. At the same instant I fired, the whale unexpectedly rolled to one side. The orca's sudden, unusual maneuver resulted in the harpoon hitting below water in the abdomen. Darn, tough luck; I hoped the animal had plenty of protective blubber there. I threw the buoys out and we followed their path.

We got a call from a Navy patrol boat, "You are entering a restricted zone reserved for submarine testing."

I responded, "We're following the killer whales, trying to catch one."

The Navy man retorted, "You take your whales and clear the area!"

The whales continued on, of course, undeterred. We detoured a bit and rejoined them.

Captain Adam Ross steered the Chinook toward the harpooned whale. Two companions joined her north of Fox Island. The trio swam toward Horsehead Bay, surfacing to breathe every five minutes. The whales altered course while submerged; but Captain Ross held close behind the whale-towed marker floats. Lamar's camera crew positioned their boat directly in the path of the whales. The water depth decreased, twenty, nineteen, eighteen fathoms; the net could reach bottom here. A group of six to eight orca surfaced between the capture vessel and the beach.

"Ted, there are at least two cows in that group," Don radioed. "We're going for them."

Black smoke poured from the stack, net peeled off the pile and flew over the stern. The seiner's power skiff dragged one end of the net toward the beach. The Chinook turned for shore; the whales surfaced inside the half-closed circle. In another minute the Chinook met its skiff, completing the circle, then overlapped both ends of the net. "Sixteen fathoms, the lead line is on bottom," Don called.

I watched for the orca inside the circle of net, hardly able to contain myself until they surfaced. How many? How big? The whale-towed buoy moved across the net enclosure. Several yards from the cork line it unexpectedly submerged. *The buoy had submerged?*

A minute later all the whales surfaced, outside the net. They must have dived under the sinking lead line. One cow was floundering, held fast by the harpoon line. Spellbound, I watched, agonizing as she battled to get free. I was emotionally tangled in her traumatic struggle, inexplicably wanting her to get away. Suddenly it was over; the harpoon pulled out of the whale's body. Freed, the female joined her waiting pod.

I radioed to Don for a new harpoon with buoys and line. Five minutes later my copter hovered over the ship's fantail. I leaned out the door, stretching for the bundle held aloft by Don. Just when I took hold of the heavy pack, a yank on my safety strap pulled me abruptly into the aircraft. The pilot's teeth were pressed together, lips parted, cheek muscles bulging. He was frantic about something. Had we hit the Chinook? As we lifted smartly away, I heard his voice an octave higher than usual, "That was close, as close as we'll ever come to losing this copter. You CAN'T lean out like that! We nearly tipped over. I had the stick hard against the stop. In another second we would have been garbage."

A second close call; a year ago I forgot to throw out the buoys. I hoped he would continue flying with me. "I apologize, Bob, I wasn't thinking."

"You're not alone in this aircraft, you know. We work as a team or not at all!"

He was right. I had to think more about the helicopter and Bob, not just what I was doing.

"How much time have I got?" I asked.

"About thirty minutes, and we are losing daylight." The whales had learned our plan and were wary, their swimming pattern unpredictable. We tried approaching a small group; the orca scattered and sounded. A second attempt was equally unsuccessful. "It's no good, Ted; it's getting dark and the whales are so spooked they dive the moment we near them."

I couldn't stand having another day end in failure. Though no orca were in sight, I said, "There's something out there, Bob." We zoomed along the shoreline searching for my phantom whales. "Look!" Two whales, surprisingly, had surfaced ahead.

"Better try for that big cow," Bob said. Still hoping for a pod bull, I hesitated. The pilot urged, "Let's wind it up, Ted; time to go home."

It's now or never I felt and, ignoring the pilot's remark, motioned to descend. The whales had submerged out of sight, but my internal guidance system would lead me to them. I pointed, indicating a slight change in course. The seconds ticked away. "Now! Bob, dive!" The animals surfaced rather far away. With a conditioned reflex, I aimed a little high over the largest distant gray form, and fired the rifle.

Bob was looking squarely at me. "Well?"

"I don't know," I answered, then began retrieving the

harpoon line. It seemed snagged and drew tight. The little nylon cord jerked in my hands; it felt alive. I was pulling, trying to haul in the biggest "fish" I had ever hooked, not even sure if the whale was on the line.

Bob was sure. He felt it in the copter's reactions. "Let go!" he shouted. "Get us free of the whale."

I tossed out the floats. Finally my exhausted mind comprehended; the whale really was harpooned, and I saw it move off towing the string of buoys.

The calm night air had a sharp edge. The whales rested in a small bay just ahead of our boat. Pete inflated a special orange buoy, sealing tight two flashlights stuffed into its center. It was a strange sight, the glowing orange ball moving gently behind the whale, surely a large pumpkin with flickering candle. The date was October 31, Hallowe'en.

The big, open-top pot came to a boil on the galley stove. Adam slid an insulator pad under the pot and casually dumped in several measures of coffee. The pungent aroma brought the crew running. They bent over the hot cups, warming their fingers. "We're going to do some business, Buster; I just know it," Adam said. "We didn't catch them yesterday because the net was dry and sank too slowly. Tomorrow we'll wet it down." Adam was as eager to catch a whale as any man I knew.

I learned that Adam and his friend Peter Babich had been the fellows who called the Canadian fishermen, telling them Ted Griffin might buy their trapped killer whales. In trying to discuss how he would make tomorrow's set on the orca, I got cut off in mid-sentence with Adam's curt, "I'll just do it. Never you mind how."

At first light the whales swam unhesitatingly into Henderson Bay, quite a contrast from their refusal to enter Quartermaster Harbor. However, this time the water became shallow on a gradual slope.

"What do you make of it, Ted, only two?"

"I don't know. Maybe they've been abandoned by the pod. At least we have a chance to catch a companion for Namu and if we're lucky, we'll catch the other whale as well."

Two purse seiners followed the orange marker float. I had chartered the second one hoping two vessels could work together. The Chinook moved ahead and was abreast of the whales when they surfaced. The back-up vessel remained in a pre-arranged position.

"Twelve fathoms," Don called out; "let her go." Steaming at nine knots, top speed for the Chinook, the seiner released its net. The whales, sensing the sudden barrier, tried to outrun the ship. The speed boats raced ahead and forced the surfacing whales back. With one third of the net out, the seiner heeled over in a ninety degree turn and headed toward the beach. The whales' escape was cut off in two directions; the buoy indicated they had doubled back. A minute later Adam's six-hundred-fathom net was all used up, lying in a giant "U" shape. The skipper on the second seiner released his net, heading straight across the open end of Adam's. Like putting the keeper plate on a horse-shoe magnet, SNAP, the escape route closed.

Adam's slow, emotion-filled voice broke over the CB, "Inside, boys, they're inside the net."

We watched the two whales slowly settle down. The large cow and a smaller animal, perhaps her calf, adopted a circular swimming pattern. Neither appeared distressed, nor made any attempt to get out. Don and I, eager for a close inspection, paddled a boat inside the enclosure. When the animals swam very close to us, Don leaned over the side and cut the harpoon line and buoys away from the cow. "Well, Ted, we got a mate for Namu, and a little one in the bargain. You're going to have your hands full in Rich Cove."

"Yeah, it will be quite an adjustment for me and

Namu. The large cow is sort of a mail-order bride."

Lamar came up to the nets and called, "Ted, that was really exciting action. The first capture of a live killer whale and it's all on film!"

The seiner crews stood along the rails and atop the pilot houses, silently watching the animals. Two speed boats, the sea plane, and the helicopter were all tethered in a string behind the Chinook, snaking in the light breeze.

Don and I scrounged a few big anchors and strategically placed them to prevent the net from collapsing inward around the whales. I had hired Gary Keffler and Dale Dean to help with the underwater work. They arrived within several hours and immediately checked the entire net, reporting, "It's on bottom all the way around. There are no holes, everything looks good."

I asked Dale, "Do you hear the whales talking down there?"

"Yeah, a little squeak now and then."

The boats and planes had attracted considerable attention. Local inhabitants were gathering to watch. Others who heard us talking on the CB radios soon converged on the scene. A pleasure boater asked, "Are those killer whales?"

"Sure are. Want to pet one?"

"No sirree. Ah, OK if we watch?"

"That's fine, but please don't tie your boat to the net."

Catching the whales had taken all my ingenuity, more money than the movie producer put up, and more energy than I could have imagined. It had been a monumental week-long effort and we were all nearly exhausted.

Newspaper and TV reporters arrived. Among them I saw Bruce McKim of the *Seattle Times* who had journeyed with Namu to Seattle. He said, "Hello, Ted, I see you have been busy. Those are fine looking animals. How big are they? What are your plans for them?"

"My guess is the cow will go twenty feet or more. The little one may be fourteen feet. The big whale is a companion for Namu, if they get along."

"Is that her calf?" the photographer asked.

"I don't know; haven't seen it try to nurse."

As the first streaks of sunlight crossed the water, a tug entered Henderson Bay towing Namu's travel pen. Once the pen was positioned Gary and Dale worked underwater securing it to the net containing the whales.

"All set, tiger," Dale said. "They have a doorway thirty feet by thirty feet."

A lightweight net was placed behind the two whales, then slowly drawn in, forcing them to the pen's door. I was shaking uncontrollably. They were most likely to break out or become tangled when crowded like this. Don's voice was loud, forceful, masking his tension, "OK, a little more, easy, easy." The two whales dove, in a line, swimming straight into the pen.

Gary and Dale jumped in the water, grabbed the net door, and pulled it to the surface. They repeated the lacing sequence that I had done on Namu's net in Warrior Cove, then Gary called, "All buttoned up, ready to travel."

"How do they look?" I asked.

"It's kind of tight in there for two, but they are doing fine."

To me they resembled ballet dancers. In the cramped quarters their movements were graceful and majestic.

"What are your plans now, Ted?" Lamar asked.

"We'll be towing the pen all night; should be at the cove early in the morning. Do you want to film the transfer?"

"Sure do, I'll see you then. Good luck."

The second seiner, having recovered its net, began towing the pen to Rich Cove. At twilight the tag-along spectators headed for port, one by one. With Pegasus tied alongside the pen, Don and I concentrated on the large animal. She had developed trouble swimming. It was dark and hard to see clearly. The cow was listing, her breathing irregular. "Don, look! Bubbles emerging from her side. She's wounded."

"That must be the same animal you harpooned several days ago, the one that broke free when the buoy line tangled in the net."

"She's getting weaker. Call the ship; tell them to stop towing and get back here."

The huge mammal floundered and washed against the back of the pen. Don and I, fully clothed, jumped into the forty-seven degree water, no time for wet suits. We secured lines around the pectoral fins, cinched up, and lashed her to the perimeter log. She labored to breathe. The little whale tried to remain near the cow.

The towing vessel maneuvered alongside. "What's wrong?"

"The cow is . . . dying." I said it without having consciously accepted that prognosis. We struggled to hold her blowhole up. I felt the whale relax; she settled underwater. Don gave a mighty heave, lifting the three ton animal until its blowhole was above water, and hollered at me, "Take up the slack! Tie her off."

In a daze, my strength ebbing with the life of the whale, I was little help to Don. The ship's crew lowered the boom over the animal. Don shouted to them, "Get a line to her, quick!" The whale was frothing about the mouth. With a sudden violent convulsion, she tore loose, opened her blowhole, and plunged her head underwater. The enormous body went limp before the lifting line could raise her. I was too emotionally wrung out and exhausted to speak. The long-faced crew of the seiner hovered quietly at the rail, baffled, unable to help. Numb with pain, I refused to accept the animal's death, yet knew full well she was dead.

Killer whales are so special. The death of even one was an agonizing price to pay for being among the first to attempt capturing them alive, and not knowing the best way to proceed. It was little consolation, but I had read that in the early days of jungle animal capture as many as ten died for each one brought back alive, and they had experience.

Capturing whales was dangerous for man and animal, yet I believed it important in gaining further knowledge about the little-understood, and often-maligned, killer whale.

With the aid of the ship, the orca was lifted out of the pen. I checked the mammary glands for signs of lactation. She appeared dry; the small whale was not dependent. I asked Don, "How much water have we got right here?"

"Hitting seventy fathoms."

"What do you think?"

"That's plenty deep, Ted. She'll stay down." Weighted by anchor and chain, the whale sank to the bottom. Deeply troubled over the death of the whale, I made the choice to conceal the loss, not wanting to arouse adverse public opinion.

The young killer whale was alone, perhaps for the first time in its life. During the long night tow, I played the searchlight across the pen every few minutes, concerned. I could easily see the whale in the clear water. Without the cow for comparison the calf looked larger, almost grown up. It did not shy from the light, or show any evidence of fear. The young orca was far more agile than Namu; turning very fast somersaults, roll-overs, banking to one side, then the other. It "flew" gracefully through the water like a glider. Every minute or so the animal surfaced; the sound of its breathing strong and forceful. Quicker and higher-pitched than Namu's, the breathing sounds reflected the whale's younger age and smaller size. It was going to be fun to watch the two orca together in the lagoon.

16
Shamu

We arrived at Rich Cove before dawn. With the engine shut down, all was quiet in the pass. A dog's faint bark drifted out to us, seeming a hundred miles away. Namu squeaked an ephemeral sound, as though answering. The calf rested on the surface as Namu often would. It made no audible sound.

At daylight we began the transfer. Namu watched while we connected the calf's travel pen to the gate in the Rich Cove net. It appeared curiosity was his motive. I thought it unusual that no conversation was taking place between the two orca, not so much as a click or a squeal.

By the time the underwater door was opened, Namu had wandered away. With a second of hesitation, the small whale dashed through and surfaced a minute later at the farthest possible distance from Namu. For the remainder of the day the calf never ventured near him. How totally unexpected, as though they were different animal species from different worlds. However, Namu's apparent shyness didn't cause him to miss feeding time.

The morning following the arrival I drove to the cove early. The little whale was vocalizing; the calls feeble, almost like human crying. Namu floated upside down, mouth open, in front of me. Holding a salmon in each hand, I brushed him with one fish, keeping his attention, then tossed the other to the calf. The young orca ignored the food. Namu was content taking hand-outs. Further attempts to feed the new animal failed. Had Namu intimidated the small whale? Maybe it didn't eat because of trauma and unfamiliar surroundings. I had no way of knowing.

Namu finished breakfast and headed toward the calf. Both whales were out of sight for several minutes, then surfaced at opposite sides of the cove. I figured Namu had scrounged up all the fish tossed to the calf.

I put on my wet suit and joined Namu for a little play, teasing him with a large salmon. Holding it just out of reach excited him. Unsuccessfully trying to outmaneuver me, he resorted to shoving, a little, then faster and faster. I couldn't dislodge myself from his snout. Mask and fins fell away, cold water poured through my suit. The instant I released the fish, the whale released me. A few seconds later Namu came back and offered a ride to the float. There I put on a spare mask and fins.

When I rejoined Namu with salmon in hand, the young whale swam nearby. The bull took the fish and chomped, cutting it in three parts. Taking hold of the belly portion lightly between two teeth, he shook his head, spilling the entrails, definitely a new behavior. In a flash the young whale streaked by and scooped up the salmon parts. I was amazed, and quickly offered Namu a succession of fish. He repeated the behavior with each food offering. I was relieved to have the calf eating on only her second day. The following day the young orca approached the feed station, but would not come closer while the large one was present. In between courses, on the breaks Namu normally took during meals, he swam toward the calf with a fish; the strange, chomp-and-shake-apart feeding behavior repeated.

Later Namu seemed asleep, floating high and drifting, fifty yards away. The little whale surfaced at the feed platform; cautiously I slipped it a small chunk of salmon. The whale took the food and darted away, like a squirrel scurrying off to eat a nut in private. Several minutes later she was back. I held a fish above water; the young whale awkwardly reached for the morsel. Opening wide, the lower jaw was under water. I trailed the fish across her forehead, saying, "Roll over, like Namu does. Come on, there, over, over you go." The baby whale learned, in only a few minutes, that opening its jaw while upside down facilitated taking food held above water. Namu came over to investigate the commotion. This time the youngster held her ground, ignoring Namu's presence, and put away one hundred pounds of salmon by day's end.

I speculated on the curious initial meals. Was this how a young killer whale was weaned? Did it indicate a feeding hierarchy of a killer whale pod? Did it mean something else altogether, or nothing? I did not find the answer in later years of observation.

"Watch this, Jim." I tossed a small salmon to the center of the lagoon. Namu tried to get there first, but was outmaneuvered. "The bull got the little one started eating his leftovers the day after it arrived."

"That's remarkable, seeing how it took Namu a long time to begin eating regularly. What are your plans for the new whale? Is it a female?"

"I think so but it will be a few years before she is old enough to be a suitable mate. For now, they seem to be getting along."

"Any progress on your new aquarium at Seattle Center?"

"Oh, that's become quite a controversial issue. Suddenly there is support for a youth center to be located at the proposed aquarium site. The *P.I.* has me pitted against the young people; seems I'm an ogre, taking away something from the kids."

"I know. I've been reading some of the stories. It's too bad. If that falls through, what are you going to do with the whales? You can't put them back in that polluted Elliott Bay."

"I don't yet have the answer."

"How are your finances? Did Ivan Tors cover all your whale-capture expenses?"

"Yeah, most of them; I owe about five thousand."

"And Namu's costs, bringing him to Seattle and all?"

"Haven't paid everyone yet. I'll catch up when Namu returns to Seattle in the spring."

"How are you covering expenses now?"

"I have something like an open account at the bank. They are a little nervous, yet go along with me. They'd never admit it, but I think they view the killer whale as a kind of collateral."

Jim knelt on the wet dock, reaching for the young whale. Namu tried to barge in for some attention. The calf pushed the big orca and nuzzled Jim's hand.

"You ever think about becoming a whale trainer?" I asked.

"Not seriously, one in the family is enough."

I guess he was right about that.

During the next few days the little whale grew bolder, joining Namu and me while we played. When I left the water the calf teased the big bull, trying to get him to chase her. The water would boil around them when they had an occasional frolic. The young one often followed Namu and attempted to duplicate his actions, comical in her attempts. When the large whale jumped for a fish suspended on a long pole, the calf at first followed alongside, then later tried to get there first. The two orca began "talking" to one another more and more.

One day I called to Namu as usual; he answered and came over. The little one was silent and swam to the far side of the lagoon. When I was astride Namu, the calf came near and I tried to pet her. Each time I leaned over, the baby ducked away, then swam circles around us, more and more rapidly. In another minute she darted away for no apparent reason.

Next morning Namu appeared with teeth marks down his spine. Later I saw the calf open her mouth and rake him, but the big bull paid no heed.

One afternoon the little whale circled Namu and me, darting away and racing back, uttering high-pitched shrieks of long duration, bubbles streaming from her blowhole. From below, the young animal rammed Namu, forcing him up and nearly dislodging me. It happened so fast there was no time to react. Namu seemed unaffected. The little orca went off by herself. A while later she was back, bobbing her head up and down, making fast passes in front of us. Then she disappeared.

Wham! The calf came out of nowhere and butted Namu's side. Streaking away, she returned and struck another blow. I jumped from Namu's back, the float only several yards distant. Now the smaller whale came at ME, full speed. I tucked into a protective ball; the little orca struck me a glancing blow. With a scramble I reached the safety of the float, my shoulder feeling numb where she hit me.

When the fright abated, I was troubled by new thoughts. Would I be able to return to Namu? Were the young whale's actions simply playful, adolescent behavior; or did they develop from a more sinister motive—jealousy? If it continued I would have to partition the cove.

During the filming sequences the young orca took no notice of the various people in and out of the water. Just in case, someone usually kept her occupied at the food station. Although she occasionally threatened, no one was molested. It seemed I was the problem.

Several days later the small whale attacked again while I was astride the bull. I stepped from Namu's back directly onto the float, out of danger. When I was no longer in the water the calf calmed down and came to the float, allowing me to pet her.

Gone were my carefree days of horseplay with Namu. Had the young whale rammed me as she had the bull, I'd probably have been killed. And I could only assume that might be her next move. In planning for a second whale, and possible mate for Namu, I had expected to interact freely with both animals. This new development was quite a disappointment.

"Look," said Jim, "you can solve several problems by selling that second whale. It was the little animal trapped with Namu that the other buyers had wanted in Warrior Cove. There'll be funds to carry you over the winter, and part of the money to build temporary facilities at your aquarium; with only one whale you won't have to build quite as large a pool. Next year you can find a proper mate for Namu, and start that oceanarium."

Jim was talking sense and whether from fear, or jealousy, or both, I wanted that little whale away from Namu. I made inquiries.

The first few answers were negative: "No thank you, we have pilot whales." And, "We intend to capture our own killer whale." And, "I'm afraid our facilities couldn't handle an animal that size."

Then one showed interest. An oceanarium called Sea World had recently opened in southern California. I knew little about them, though they were very competitive with the place I used to visit, Marineland of the Pacific near Los Angeles. I flew to San Diego and looked over their facilities. Overall, the marine park was bright and cheerful;

winding paths led through landscaped, tropical gardens to secluded displays of marine mammals, birds, and fish. Most important, the animals were healthy, active, attentive, in full color. They seemed as much at home there as I was.

The animal hospital and veterinary facilities were the finest I had ever seen. Sea World's philosophy was to invest heavily in their animals' health rather than continually replace them. The initial high cost expended in housing and training their animals could be justified when they lived near-normal life spans. In the future, should an animal's habitat be threatened or destroyed, full knowledge might allow their continued propagation in captivity, and their continued participation in the balance of life.

We struck a bargain, though a highly unusual one. They would lease the killer whale by the month. Neither of us knew the value of the orca to them, nor how long it would live. None, including Namu, had ever lived more than a few months in captivity. I thought if anyone could succeed, it would be Sea World. The shared-risk approach was a good one.

"She looks good, Ted. A fine animal. Are you sure about the sex?" asked the veterinarian.

"That's what I've assumed, but there's no guarantee."

"I'll make certain when she's beached for the medical exam."

"Medical exam?" I asked.

"Yes, Sea World wants a certified healthy whale." Dr. David Kenny had arrived in mid-December. He estimated the animal's measurements and designed a steel shipping cradle fitted with a canvas sling to support the fourteen foot whale on the trip to San Diego.

Separating the calf from the bull on shipping day was a bit tricky. The young whale, recently certified a female and named "Shamu", tried to remain with Namu. After various attempts we finally tossed two fish simultaneously. That separated the whales. We then quickly drew a four-hundred-foot long net between them. Shamu darted along the corkline. Namu appeared anxious, but did not interfere until the small whale, now beached, cried out, then he came after us. Running aground in the shallow water, he was forced to stop.

Jerry Brown stroked the calf, speaking gently to her. The diver knew control was important; a frightened whale could submerge her blowhole and accidently drown. Incredibly, Shamu became calm in the midst of confusion. Jerry said, "Hey, Ted, she understands. We're talking to each other."

"The whales are always talking, Jerry. It's only that you know how to listen."

The ten or so handlers worked the one-ton baby into a sling, each person assigned one aspect of the whale's positioning and comfort. Suspended in mid-air, the young whale gave a terrific shriek; Namu answered. A few minutes later Shamu was resting in her sling, suspended in the cradle aboard a truck.

The Vashon-Fauntleroy ferry had waited ten minutes for our arrival. Many passengers gathered around the trussed-up killer whale, which had caused the rare delay. "Imagine, a whale having to cross Puget Sound on a ferry," said one of the deckhands.

At the Seattle-Tacoma airport the representative from Flying Tiger said, "We've flown them all, every kind of animal, bird and fish, but this is our first killer whale."

Enroute to southern California aboard the chartered, swingtail aircraft, Shamu's every need was attended. She rested on sheepskin pads. Water flowed continuously on her body to prevent over-heating. We painted her head and dorsal white with zinc oxide to prevent drying and cracking of the skin. These were some of the things we had learned caring for Namu.

Aboard the aircraft the veterinarian cut away the canvas obstructing her vision, saying "Shamu wants to see what's going on, same as we would." When we moved out of her sight, she set to shrieking with such volume we had to plug our ears, and for the remainder of the journey, made sure one of us kept her company.

At Sea World in San Diego, Shamu was lowered into an oval pool filled to a depth of three feet. She was carefully unwrapped from her sheepskin padding and sling. Men in wetsuits held the whale upright and under control with bedsheets pulled under each pectoral flipper. Accidental drowning was still a possibility as she was groggy from the trip. A Pacific striped dolphin, many times smaller, easily maneuvered in the shallow water. The curious dolphin, placed with Shamu for companionship, poked around the new creature. The orca lunged for the disrespectful dolphin, and was barely restrained. With increased water depth, Shamu dragged the attendants around the pool. Finally the veterinarian said she was sufficiently recovered to be released. Almost immediately the dolphin and whale were swimming together in near-perfect unison. Watching the two of them and a diver/trainer through the glass window of the large, clear-water pool until dark, I wished I had such a fine facility for Namu.

17
Widening Circles

When my brother asked to ride Namu I was not surprised but felt apprehensive and somewhat reluctant. I didn't want to share my companion, nor jeopardize the close relationship with the orca. Namu, I felt, was a one-man animal. He might even be hostile toward another human. At times the big mammal could play rough. Hardened from years of skindiving and strenuous physical activity, I had stamina, and rolled with the whale's punches; but what about Jim? I could have said no, yet if anyone were entitled to ride the killer whale, it was Jim.

I presented him with all the risks. When he made his decision I knew that he had neither hedged his bet, nor limited his exposure. With a neoprene wetsuit his only protection, Jim joined me alongside Namu. I held the sea horse's imaginary reins, while my brother climbed the whale's back. The orca, who usually began swimming as soon as I mounted, hesitated with Jim.

He asked, "How do I make him go?"

"I guess he's confused. He hasn't had to contend with two swimmers before." Once I had left the water, Namu took Jim for a long ride around Rich Cove. For the first time I watched another person ride a killer whale. It was fascinating. Now I knew the excitement others felt watching me.

Waterproof camera in hand, I returned to the lagoon. The whale insisted on keeping his nose pressed against me. Gaining adequate distance for taking pictures was quite difficult.

When Jim climbed on the dock, I asked, "Were you scared?"

"No. Should I have been?"

I wanted to see the expression on his face, but he turned away. On purpose?

The photograph of Jim riding Namu is a little incongruous hanging on his "trophy wall", somewhere between the laundromat franchise and the state bank he organized. Looking at the row of pictures depicting achievements that might have been done by ten individuals his age, I wondered about the latest entry. An end in itself, or a stepping stone toward a higher goal?

About a week later in Seattle's Underwater Sports store, when I was picking up diving tanks, the owner asked, "Will the whale let anyone, besides you, ride him?"

"First my brother, and then Jim and John, two fellows working with Lamar on the film. What did you have in mind?"

"Just that every day I'm hounded by customers, employees, and members of the 'Mud Sharks' who all want to give it a try. You know most of them; they have collected specimens the past three years," Gary Keffler said.

Though some risk was involved, the fact that Namu allowed others to ride had convinced me he had an out-going personality. It would be very special for other people to experience the joy of interacting with a four-ton killer whale. I asked our agent, "What if several skin divers swam with Namu? Would the aquarium be liable?"

"In the insurance business, we call them uninvited guests. They do it at their own risk."

I phoned Gary at the dive shop, "I'll be at Rich Cove tomorrow, all day. Tell your friends that no one is being invited. If they happen by the cove dressed in wetsuits, well, we'll see."

"That's swell, Ted. I'm sure everyone will understand. They'll be excited to hear the news. Be sure and feed Namu an especially big breakfast."

The following day two women cautiously treaded water in the Rich Cove lagoon. Like a rental horse, Namu "stood" quietly nearby, as though he understood their apprehension. With gathering courage a man finally slipped over the dock side and joined the women. Dell had shared the shark ride with me. I guess he found the whale a little more intimidating than a shark. The neoprene-skinned, pseudo-water creatures eased closer to the whale. I marveled how they instinctively got acquainted by petting Namu. He was thoroughly enjoying the grooming. The orca blew air, then stopped before letting it all out. A diver's hand had come too close to his blowhole. The hand was quickly drawn back; the orca completed his breath cycle.

More swimmers entered the water; the whale was surrounded with attendants. Namu moved in slow-motion. I had never seen him behave so gently. He allowed as many divers as could hang on, to ride together. When he turned upside down, others sat on his belly and stood on his chin. He raised his tail and tapped it lightly, pat, pat, pat. The swimmers grabbed his flukes and held on while he lifted them gently out of the water. I thought of it as a water ballet. Each time a swimmer entered the water the whale swam to them. If someone did not mount, Namu would try to take him or her on his back, or hook them gently with a fin. "Climb on," the whale seemed to say, "there is room for all."

After filming the occasion, I jumped in the lagoon. Namu broke away from the others, like a dog leaving a litter of pups, and came directly to me. "Hey, Ted, why don't you stay out of the water. That's the only way Namu will play with us." Reluctantly I returned to the float and watched. Namu was rounding them up like a mother hen, insisting on keeping them together.

"Ted, that killer whale is a pussycat. I don't know when I've had so much fun. The word will get out, and you'll have a thousand skin divers over here. Do you think all killer whales are like Namu? so gentle?"

"I'm sure some are, though probably not all."

That day, the first of many similar occasions, took place before Shamu had left Rich Cove, and the fun ended when she threatened the divers. Her reckless behavior with me was evidently not all due to adolescent exuberance, or jealousy. At Sea World Shamu took a while before allowing her trainer to ride. During one special performance, she grabbed the leg of a woman swimming in the pool. The orca finally released her captive who was close to drowning; the injured leg required many stitches. Shamu, apparently, was not quite the "pussycat" that Namu was.

One after another, photographers under contract to *National Geographic* streamed through Rich Cove. Then one day I received a phone call from the illustration editor, Bill Garrett. "I'm sorry, Ted," he said. "The Namu story has been dropped." I learned from Bill that the text written by someone they had hired was not sufficiently compelling, and they lacked enough good photographs. After a trip to their headquarters in Washington, D.C. they asked me to write the story, and agreed to send another photographer.

A week later a tall, slightly-built man showed up at Rich Cove and introduced himself, "Flip Schulke. I 'string' for *National Geographic*. They said I was being sent

to photograph an orca and I asked, 'What's an orca?' They replied, 'You just get on a plane and fly out there.'"

"Come on, Flip, I'll show you an orca."

Though burdened with camera cases and diving gear, my visitor moved with style and grace. He exuded vitality. I said, "You're the umpteenth photographer they've sent. Think you can get the kind of pictures they want?"

"Yeah, I think so. What kind of visibility do you have here?"

"Sunny days, ten to fifteen feet."

"Uhh, nothing to rave about. Hey, the whale's huge. How long *is* he?"

"Twenty two feet or so."

"That's going to be tough. Well, I'd like to get started."

His manner was slightly abrasive, perhaps a reflection of his self-confidence. With a glance at Lamar's shark-protection filming cage, he asked, "How safe is it, swimming with the killer whale?"

"Let's hope the animal likes you."

Flip shrugged. Feeding several fish to Namu, the man quickly became acquainted with the orca, which started nudging and playfully pushing at the photographer in the water. "He's quite a pest. How can I get him to leave me alone?"

"I'll come in; that will help."

Wearing an air tank and extra lead, Flip lay on the bottom looking up through his view finder. I maneuvered Namu above the cameraman; then played with the whale.

"Great stuff, Ted. Now some close ups."

Away from the float, I turned to face the whale; he stopped quickly. I grabbed the orca's upper lips with one hand and forced my other inside his mouth. To my amazement he allowed me to pry open his massive jaws just like a pet dog. He made no attempt to bite or pull away, taking his cues from me.

Flip and I talked over the experience. I had not really broken the ice with the man, but Namu had. Flip's voice shifted to a different key when he spoke of the whale.

National Geographic reported that the new batch of pictures and my manuscript did the trick. With Flip's special knowledge of underwater photography he was able to overcome the poor visibility by using surface light to silhouette Namu, skillfully employing a wide-angle, "fish-eye" lens. In a way, these images of the whale and me were more mysterious and exciting to look at than a clear portrait.

Following publication of my story, "Making Friends with a Killer Whale", in *National Geographic*, March, 1966, people corresponded from many parts of the world. Letters arrived loosely addressed to: The Whale Man, Captain Ahab, Namu, Seattle Aquarium, and Rich Cove, Washington, a place having no postal designation. They wrote: "Could I come to work at the aquarium? I've always loved dolphins and whales and want to train them." And, "These pictures were drawn by the fifth grade class after reading your story. The children are so eager to hear from you. Please send them a letter telling us what you have learned recently." Not all were complimentary: "It's inhumane to keep that freedom-loving whale caged. You are the animal that should be put behind bars." And, "No one should be allowed to exhibit any of God's creatures for profit."

The stack of mail was often more than I could read in a day. "I have trained dolphins and ridden them. Some day I would like to ride a killer whale. If I come to Seattle, will it be possible for me to ride Namu?" And, "I congratulate you on your accomplishments with the killer whale. Your story is the greatest man and animal adventure I have ever read."

I wrote each one, as time allowed, feeling as though I knew them, and looked forward to meeting those who made the trip to Seattle.

Perhaps it was the early hour of the Spring day, the movie actors in Rich Cove were cold, stiff, unapproachable. Last week the producer had said, "We have to wrap things up. We've been filming for five months and are way over budget."

The director glanced frequently skyward as he took me aside, "What we must do is bring Lansing and Namu together."

"You want the star to ride the whale?"

"That is what I hope, though it's uncertain that he will do it. Lansing has never seen a killer whale before today. Help him realize there is no danger."

Lamar added, "You and I know Namu acts like an overgrown puppy, but a lot of this crew are wary of him."

By mid-morning the sun had burned away the haze and shone brightly. Wearing a rib belt concealed beneath my wetsuit, I joined two of the film's stars on the far end of the float. How could I best ease the transition from killer whale-sea monster, to Namu-gentle pet?

". . . No, it's unlikely any orca would injure a human. Think of him like a horse that loves attention." *Oowwuch.* Bending over to pick up a salmon, I was stabbed with pain from three cracked ribs. While riding Namu in a jump, I had fallen off and was accidentally clobbered by his tail. "Here, Robin," I said, handing the young actress a fish, "see if Namu comes to you." I hoped she would warm to the orca when he displayed interest in her.

The whale's mouth opened, his pink tongue pressed forward, splash, slurp, "EEEE, URRH, EH."

Robin Mattson beamed, "Oh, he's fun. Can I feed Namu again?"

"You'd better, or he will be mighty disappointed."

She held another chunk of salmon aloft. A firm hand gripped my arm and drew me back; a cameraman stepped gracefully forward, his attendant elevating an unusual-looking silver umbrella. When Lee Meriwether, the lead actress, joined the group they groomed the receptive orca with the long-handled brush. Initial apprehensions were soon forgotten.

"Eeee, urrh, eh," I called. The orca quickly located me standing in shallow water.

Bob Lansing, the film's male lead, was escorted gently but firmly into the water by the director, "Just a little something with you and Namu."

The whale nuzzled the actor. I encouraged him, "He likes you; pet him; that's it, both hands, lots of physical contact." Lansing eased alongside Namu. "Go ahead, take hold of the dorsal; he won't move until you climb on."

With a small effort, the man was astride the orca; Namu headed for deep water. Lansing hunched over, head down, totally absorbed in the new experience. Then, as though someone had turned on the electricity, the veteran actor followed the director's cues; he lost his look of apprehension, straightened up, and turned toward the cameras. The faces of those watching revealed their concern; few had expected that he would actually ride the whale, thought to be a "dangerous" assignment. Lansing made it look easy; but, unknown to most, he was on a merry-go-round, which could not easily be stopped. Namu's new habit was not to release a rider willingly.

"Eeee, urrh, eh; eeee, urrh, eh. Come on, Namu," I called. As the whale approached, he sensed the man's intention to climb down, and the orca turned sharply away. "Lansing! get off, now!" I shouted. He slid from the back of the behemoth, wearing a smile of success. The whale stopped immediately and whirled around, walloping Lansing with a fluke. The actor was knocked off his feet and yanked under. I feared he had suffered a similar fate, cracked ribs, or worse.

Namu's fluke action was partly the result of the whale turning, but it was also an attempt to recapture the rider. Namu often recovered tossed fish by sculling with his fluke, causing the dead fish to "swim" forward to the whale's mouth.

Lansing struggled to the surface, visibly shaken. Jim and John, well acquainted with Namu from working on the film, leaped to assist. I occupied the whale while they pulled the star to the float. Fortunately the actor was uninjured and the final day's filming judged a complete success. The close-up, "establishing shots" were "in the can." They linked Namu with the actors who had been filming in the San Juan Islands using a manufactured killer whale.

The motion picture, *Namu the Killer Whale*, premiered in Seattle in July, 1966. Shown around the country in movie houses, it continues to appear on television.

"What are my chances for getting out of this alive?" asked the journalist, half in jest.

"Slightly better than getting your Namu story published unaltered." I had taken a gamble in granting Jim Halpin the interview. His employer, *Seattle* magazine, frequently published emotionally appealing articles slanted against business. My concern was unnecessary. The story was printed just as Halpin wrote it, fairly and objectively.

Though an unskilled diver, the journalist was courageously determined to make Namu's acquaintance, and soon was astride the killer whale. Halpin's reaction is clear from the beginning of his article:

> Frankly, I had had Namu up to *here*. Like nearly everyone else in town, I was sick to death of newspaper stories about the killer whale's capture, about his tense and troubled trip from British Columbia to Puget Sound, about his summertime incarceration at Pier 56, about the pros and cons of his winding up at the Seattle Center, about his captor's attempting to trap other whales that might keep him company . . . in short, I could get along very well, thank you, if I never heard Namu's name again. Now, to my own astonishment, I have become a convert to Namu, who puzzles and fascinates me more than I would have ever thought possible.
>
> One reason for my changed viewpoint is that I have gotten to know Namu's oddly tormented master, Ted Griffin, a spare, bespectacled man of 30 who is among the great enigmas of my acquaintance. Another reason is that I have gotten to know Namu himself.

The sophisticated, objective reporter got "hooked" on the whale. In April, 1966, *Seattle* magazine published Jim Halpin's remarkably perceptive story. To the author's credit he did quite a little digging, researching well beyond our interview.

> "I think there are two Ted Griffins," a colleague has observed. "One is a really

gallant adventurer, and the other is just a
guy who wants to make a buck so bad he
itches."

From a friend he quoted:

"Although he was a shy, quiet-spoken boy,
Ted inherited from his father a love of ex-
hibitionism which the elder Griffin gratified
by driving antique cars."

Halpin continued:

I found an almost eerie rapport between Griffin and his 10,000 pound marauder. While Griffin is guarded and sometimes curt with human beings, he is joyous
and talkative with Namu. Incredibly, his
love is reciprocated. Griffin has only to
whistle—and Namu comes dashing to him
wagging a 10-foot tail that could smash a
cabin cruiser to splinters with one blow.

At the last possible second, Namu
dived slightly; that impossibly great body
swept under mine, and the next minute I
was hoisted above water, astride his back
and clutching his five-foot dorsal fin. I had
not mounted the animal; he had, with
astonishing skill, picked *me* up.

Whale riding, once you get over the
initial terror, beats horseback riding all hollow. The whale is not only a lot smarter
than a horse but far more concerned for
your safety. Namu, for example, is careful

to keep the part of him you happen to be riding close enough to the surface so that you can breathe through your snorkel. Furthermore, Namu actually *enjoys* being ridden—why, I can't imagine. He seemed sorry when I got off.

Before he left Rich Cove the day of his ride, Halpin said to me, "I found the Namu nobody knows and I'm glad I did."

18
Boy On A Dolphin

Standing on the float at Rich Cove I waved my arms and shouted, "Come on, Namu, take me for a ride." No response. I leaped in and swam toward him. "Hey, wait up." Cautiously I splashed a fish on the water, like shaking oats in a can to lure my seahorse. But the animal kept his distance.

"E-E-E-E-E," he shrieked, his head bobbing up and down in menacing, leave-me-alone fashion. He didn't relent. I swam back to the float feeling dejected.

When I returned to Seattle later that day Homer asked, "How are things with you and Namu?"

"Oh, fine," my voice trailed off, unable to conceal my disappointment. "We have our little ups and downs."

"Sounds like something is the matter. Off his feed? The honeymoon over?"

"No, no, not that; he's just acting differently."

"How?"

"This morning he wouldn't let me within twenty feet. Just kept moving away like I had the plague."

"So you automatically think it's Namu's fault?"

"What else?"

"I think it's your state of mind. You're telegraphing your feelings to the whale. There are days when you upset everyone, charging through here like a rampaging bull. Now that you're puffed with importance, making a movie, entertaining big shots, the Ted I knew is gone."

"Ah, Homer, I'm no different."

"You may not recognize the change, and maybe you

180

can fool other people, but not me, nor apparently Namu. I've spent most of my life with animals, observing and learning from them. They're very sensitive to attitude and mood, in people and one another. Slow down, get back to your regular self. You have empathy for animals. I've seen the magic you can work with them."

"I hear you, Homer, thanks."

Perhaps I was a bit impatient and sometimes curt. Recently friends had remarked I was acting like a bulldozer in high gear. Homer could be right. There were many troubles gnawing at me. Each one required time and energy. I was away from home too much. Though I had put Don Goldsberry in charge of the aquarium to gain time, I felt stressed with our disagreements over management policies. My attempt to build a new aquarium had stalled. I was such a bundle of nerves, no wonder Namu did not want to associate with me. In *Seattle* magazine, Jim Halpin wrote:

> Indeed some highly influential citizens insist that Griffin's piscatory pursuits could well blight the city's destiny. If Namu is eventually installed in a marine park . . . that would torpedo the chances of building a science-oriented aquarium, which is essential for Seattle's emergence as a chief center of oceanographic research. (Their argument presupposes not only that Puget Sound is the only sea in miniature to be found in the western hemisphere, but that, even among scientists, competition from Namu would be hard to beat.)
>   . . ."the proposed aquarium would cloud the whole issue when it comes to

getting financial support for a true research facility."

The log boom, important for keeping boats and their
propellers away from the Rich Cove net, had broken from
one of the moorings. I gathered repair gear and stuffed it
under my wetsuit jacket. I was tired, and feeling the strain
of a long day, had not wanted to enter the chilly water.
Unwilling to jump in as usual, I walked slowly out from
shore. The cold water seeped into my suit, inch by inch,
prolonging the suffering.

My body gradually warmed the liquid trapped in the
suit. Underwater, I welcomed the wonderful liberation of
weightlessness, and began the long swim; entranced, as
always, by the beauty in the fluid motion of the sea creatures. The thoughts and troubles of a busy world were left
behind with the solace of my silent, friendly undersea
garden. My mind became clear for the tasks ahead.

The swiftly-running current tugged while I crawled
along the rocky bottom dragging a heavy chain. In the half
light I searched through a jungle of broad-leaf marine
growth. An amber flag of kelp streamed overhead, growing from a steel rod running through a cement-filled drum.
I snaked a leg around the rod and pulled, gaining just
enough slack to reconnect the chain and cement anchor.
Then I used Adam's advice; "A little wire tied through the
shackle eye, like so, it won't come loose again." The log
boom was securely back in place. Though a small task, it
helped me attain a peaceful state of mind; in the quietness
under the sea, I was restored.

Reaching the corkline in darkness, I climbed over and
wondered, *Where are you, whale?* We were not on speaking
terms, and his behavior was something of a mystery. He
ate well enough, but that was the extent of our interaction.

I wanted to play with Namu again, for everything to be the same as before. I pictured in my mind how he had come when I called, and taken me on his back, as though for his pleasure. He had been gentle and friendly, quick to respond to my slightest touch.

I was shaking as I hung onto the corkline, whether from cold or fright or sadness I couldn't tell. I wanted to know what Namu was thinking, how he was feeling. His avoidance troubled me. I listened a while longer and heard him blow some distance away. Good, he wasn't coming. I swam slowly toward the distant float, then thought, *maybe I shouldn't be here,* and started racing back toward the corkline. Thump!

"Uuhh! Namu. You nearly scared me to death." In a reflex action, arms flew over my ducked head, ready for attack. *No possibility of escaping him.* When nothing happened, I slowly uncoiled and gingerly reached out, groping like a blind man. *Can't see, but I know you're there. I'm scared; I've lost confidence in our rapport. Say something. What do you want? What part of you is this? Chin? You're upside down?* Treading water, and fending off the wall of orca, I eased my way toward the float. "How did you know I was crossing through? Hear me? Telepathy?" With a little pat on his forehead I pushed him gently away and climbed on the float. "See you tomorrow, big fellow, rrr, eee, rrr, eee."

"EEE, URRH, EH."

"Rrr, eee, rrr, eee."

"EEE, URRH."

"No, no, rrr, eee, rrr, eee, rrr, eee,"

"RRR, EEE, RRR, EEE, RRR, EEE."

"Hey, that's it! Now you're talking." I started crying and didn't want to leave, feeling the same as the first time he spoke to me. It was like a door had opened when none was visible; and instantly I knew we were together again.

I had waited for the ferry Kalakala's approach. It was noisy as ever. Her klankity, klankity engine sound was nearly unbearable; it always made me feel like I was being crushed when underwater. No wonder Namu went slightly beserk. That day he shrieked as the Kalakala thundered past. Hopefully the racket concealed the sound of my entry into the water. Thirty feet below, hiding behind a large boulder with my back to the net, I called teasingly to the orca, "eee." *Now he knows I'm in the water. Can he find me?* The waiting was nerve wracking. Though I had hyperventilated before submerging, my lungs already cried for air. I had not worn air tanks because he might hear the hiss.

Maybe I should call again. Click-click-click. The sound, like striking stones together, snapped me to attention; he was looking for me alright. *Nice try, fellow, but sonar can't "see" through rock.* Creak-creak-creak, pop, pop, pop. His squeaking sounded like someone opening the gate to Dracula's castle. About sixty seconds had passed. Hunching lower, tilting my head back, I caught no sign of him in the bright circle of sunlight. I tingled all over, muscles twitching, the urge to breathe nearly driving me out of hiding.

Something was crawling up my back! AAAWKKK! I jerked with a convulsion, then whirled. Namu! He was hovering overhead, snout down, pectorals outstretched, the gigantic body curving into the surface light. He prodded again. Had I aggravated him? Maybe he was pleased to find me in our game of hide-and-seek. I couldn't tell. Namu's expression never changed. The blowhole contorted to a convoluted hump. As the muscular tissue undulated, tiny bubbles streamed forth, "EEEEEE, RRRRRR, EEEEEE. EEEEEE, RRRRRR, EEEEEE." The power of the eerie sounds set every cell in my body in tingling motion.

I slid my hands along his back, then reaching upward, grasped his dorsal. *Giddy up, whale, my lungs are on fire!* The steed bolted for the surface.

In learning to perceive the whale's little nuances, my understanding of him grew. If Namu should swim to the feed station and wait without rolling upside-down, it often meant he wanted companionship and was requesting a massage. Rapid bobbing of the head, up and down, often accompanied by a string of shrill, short squeals, indicated a mood of protest or discontent. Slow swings of the head, from side to side, accompanied by arching of the back, showed a willingness to play. Now and then he raced back and forth across the lagoon, coming out of the water in a long, low arc. Seconds later he was cruising under the float on his side, looking up. After four or five minutes of this behavior, he would stop, and swim casually back. The pattern seemed to burn off excess energy. I called it "full of beans." If I entered the water at such a time, he became a perfect gentleman.

My mood swings were reflected in the orca's temperment, especially obvious the past few weeks. Gradually I was learning the tremendous importance of my own state of mind. Often I repeated activities and play with slight variations in order to gain further understanding, but when I was distracted, I treated him like a plow horse, mechanically repeating old behavior. He didn't seem to mind. Nevertheless, everytime we had a break-through, when I really got somewhere with the whale, it was because I had shut out all interference: people, noise, any extraneous thoughts. Focusing on the whale, I then knew exactly what I wanted and visualized how it might occur.

Physical contact between us provided non-verbal communication. He responded to caresses, growing calm and gentle. At the same moment, excitement was building in me, like holding a charge in a capacitor. My feelings blossomed into joy. Namu shared it, the electricity between us, the sensation of touch, the satisfaction of contact. Lifting my hand away discharged the euphoric high. When Namu's belly was being stroked, he remained completely passive, but without my touch he turned suddenly active seeking to renew the connection.

I was concerned that Namu's intelligence would cause him to become bored. When no one was interacting with the whale he drifted at the surface, often for hours at a time, which is not common in the wild. Any activity I could work out for Namu semed to liven him up. It reminded me of the seals and sea lions that would get easily bored and lethargic. I enjoyed keeping them alert by throwing fish into the pool unannounced, and playing hide-and-seek.

Namu and Rich Cove were frequently host to out-of-town visitors who were often dressed in gray flannel suits, narrow ties, and wing-tip shoes. Their questions revealed how little they knew about whales. I understood why, but couldn't resist leading them on.

"Please stand back from the edge," I said, "wouldn't want anyone hurt. No one knows for certain if killer whales attack humans, but one crunch, that's all it would take." All eyes searched for the orca. "Like any wild animal, this bull could suddenly turn against his captors." The lagoon's surface was quiet. Through the underwater speaker I called in a sharp voice, "Hey, whale, get over here if you want something to eat." Any words would do; Namu responded to the faint electronic click of the mike switch. I held a fish high above water; no one saw the whale until he lunged from the blue-green depths. I jumped back, feigning astonishment, and shouted angrily,

"Now cut that out! You trying to take my arm off? Well, I sure won't take a chance by going in the water today." The visitors' expressions rapidly switched from anticipation to disappointment, and then grave concern.

Namu rose again for the extended salmon which I held firmly. The four-ton behemoth grabbed the fish, pulling me off balance. "Oh, no!" I shouted. Plunging into the water nearly atop the whale, I frantically swam for shore, street clothes concealing a wet suit. Namu bolted upright, exhaled, blasting the startled guests, and immediately lunged after me. In three seconds the killer was doing fifteen knots, his dorsal slicing the water in a menacing fashion; violent death appearing imminent. Swimming over my back he would crash dive, plunging me to the bottom. Pinned beneath the mountain of blubber, I often felt panic, though I knew elation would sweep over me in a moment. As before, the orca lifted off, then waited for me to mount.

Signaled with a low dorsal squeeze, Namu swam, remaining submerged. In the shadow of the float, a slight tug on the dorsal tip brought us bolting to the surface. I could see expressions of fear fade to smiles. Standing on the orca's back, it was a quick step to the dock. "Take me to your leader," I said, cracking up in laughter.

"I thought the whale was killing you! You rotten so and so, but that was the greatest show I've ever seen, just incredible. It was a trick, wasn't it? You weren't in any real danger?"

"Just show biz, fellows. Tickets please."

"Griffin, will you be serious for a minute. How did you get the whale to do all that?"

"We sort of anticipate each other's moves, and make things up as we go along."

"Does he know you from other people?"

"Let's find out. He certainly does in the water."

Namu watched each individual and twosome walk along the float. Though others remained behind, only when I departed did the whale follow, precisely by my side.

The whale played with a piece of driftwood; I coaxed him to bring the stick to the float. Anticipating my toss, he was nearly halfway to the hunk of wood before it splashed. He pushed it underwater with his chin and was delighted when it bobbed to the surface. Food reward lured him back, and we played the game again. I tossed a bright orange ball and a slab of salmon together, as I had done two years before in teaching the sea lions to retrieve rings. At first I had to dive in and bring the ball back, but within several days Namu would reliably retrieve the ball whenever it was thrown.

When I left the two-foot sphere floating in the lagoon, Namu took it in his mouth, jumping in the air. By day's end the ball was punctured with tooth holes. A replacement filled with styrofoam solved the problem and was equally popular.

He soon learned some objects were for training and must not be held in the mouth. The sight of anyone taking the orange ball up the ladder sent Namu to the far end of the lagoon. Extending the sphere from the tower was the signal. He rose halfway out of the water from one hundred yards away, took a bearing on the ball, and began his high-speed dash. As he leaped eighteen feet high, batting the ball with his nose, a good-sized wave washed over the float. Moments later he collected his reward. It was uncanny how he could travel all that way underwater, blind to his target, and reach it every time. I have observed many cetaceans using the same technique of taking a "fix" on a distant object they intended to jump for.

Arriving at Rich Cove one winter morning, I saw the killer whale submerged, but his tail was swinging around in small circles just above the surface. He reminded me of a wagging-tailed dog grousing around a rabbit hole. Perhaps he was hungrily trying to pluck a gilled fish out of the net. He greeted me halfway across the lagoon, bobbing his head. I sensed he was smiling. Namu rushed back to his spot.

Swimming to the corkline, I asked him, "OK, what's going on here?" He made short, shrill bursts of sound. I submerged, searching the net; the whale swam alongside. "Come on, Namu, there's nothing here. The fish got away; and I don't want you getting accidentally tangled."

"EEE, URRH, E-E-E-E-E. URRH, E-E-E-E."

"You don't say. OK, if you're so determined, I'll have another look." Taking several deep breaths, I dove to the bottom and found a dogfish. *You wouldn't eat one of those. Hey, where's the net?* There was a hole twenty feet wide. Nothing remained but frazzled fibers. *But how?* Then I saw. Like a giant net-eater, a three-foot-thick, barnacle-encrusted log had caught and rolled along the lead line, slashing the nylon. Had Namu been waiting for the opening to get larger, to escape? It was plenty big already. *Why haven't you—never mind; come on.* We surfaced together; however, when he would not accompany me to the float I got worried, dove again, and cinched up and knotted several torn strands of net, partially blocking the potential exit.

Namu was watching the ever-widening hole when I returned with an air supply, and fishermen's needles threaded with nylon twine. How large a door did a whale need anyway? He poked his head slightly into the gap, but did not follow when I swam through. I cut many strands of netting, releasing the water-soaked log.

"EEE, EEE, EEE."

"Eee, eee, eee yourself. Get outa here!" Waving my arms and pounding on his snout only got him to stick out his tongue. "And sassy, too. What a whale."

"EEEE-E-E-E." Namu disappeared to breathe. At least there was something I could do in the water that he couldn't, remain submerged for an hour. To get rid of the old log I grabbed the end. It was easy to lift, but required a powerful shove to move the seventy-foot deadhead into the channel. "And don't come back." I spent another hour lacing the hole closed.

As I rested, arms draped over the corkline, Namu came close. "Were you planning to leave through that hole in the net?" I asked.

Namu brought his face within inches of mine and lifted his head, almost imperceptively.

"Do you want your freedom? If I let you go, would you come back?"

I felt strongly that he would, yet lacked the courage to actually do it.

While the empty tank was being boosted to the float, Namu swam in small circles, tapping his pectoral flipper, waiting impatiently for me to rejoin him.

"Come, come, let me see them." I probed with my fingers, then tugged on his lips. "Open up, that's it." I drew my knuckles across his teeth like rapping a stick on a wood slat fence. Two months ago when I placed my hands near his eyes he had squinted and turned away; now they remained open, unflinching. "Trust me a little more, do you?"

The whale seemed to have pretty fair vision, and often watched me while I worked underwater. Exposed to salt water, my eyes blurred. But a protective mucus constantly flowed from Namu's eyes. Above water it made him look like he was crying.

Swimming with a twenty-gallon garbage pail half full of fish, I placed it on the bottom and removed the lid. Namu followed closely, inspecting the pail; and pressed his face firmly against the opening, unable to reach the food. I wondered if he would feel frustrated, and try various maneuvers such as pushing over the pail. He hovered about a foot above the top, and snapped his jaws in such a way as to create a water current. One by one, the fish slipped out of the bucket and into his mouth, as smoothly as if by magic.

His back rose; his tail pounded the water. "You demand a massage?" My fingers pressed against his firm, smooth skin, drifted down his spine, searching for the little spots which brought him pleasure. The lengthy full-body rubdown had begun. I never tired of our frequent interaction. Each time it brought us closer, forging my link with the whale.

The still night air, laden with mist, carried the faint sound of Namu's whimper. I supposed he was dreaming. I sat trying to relax, feeling a little guilty for not being home with my family. In a way I thought Namu and the wild whales had become a second family. Strange ideas and images filled my mind: undefined shadows moving in the dark of night, the haunting sounds of the whales calling me. My arms felt heavy as though weights were holding them down. When trying to visualize Namu I heard his voice, "Come with me, far away. I'll show you my world and the secret places which all orca know. In time, you'll be one of us."

When I awoke I heard the whisper of waves touching the shore. For a while the comfort of the easy chair wouldn't release me. My dream had been of a journey with Namu. We had crossed the ocean together, stopping only once when a great white shark threatened us. Namu had protected me, taking the monster in his mouth and crushing it. All the time we were together I could hear him talk to me. Though neither of us uttered a sound, somehow I knew what he was thinking, and he had answered my thoughts.

I rose from the chair, walked to the cabin doorway, and saw Namu several yards away. With a slight tail movement he was holding himself against the shore. Seeing me in the floodlight, Namu swung his head from side to side. I felt him beckoning, drawing me out the door to be with him. I hesitated, resisting as though having to make a difficult choice. Inside me a storm was growing. Namu was doing something to me, turning me inside out. I was afraid, afraid to make a choice, or even think about it. If I went to him that night, it could mean never turning back. In my mind's eye I stared into the faces of my wife and two children. Joan stretched out her arms and pleaded, "Ted, please, please come home. We love you. Don't leave us. Don't go away with Namu."

Was the choice really so clearcut? I thought of the old tale of selling one's soul to the devil in order to gain both sides of the coin. Well, I wanted everything, the whale and my family.

Wearing extra lead weights, I held my breath and dove to the bottom of the lagoon. I now attempted activities with Namu inconceivable even a few days go; since that night when he called me to his side, and I had yielded, whatever the price.

Lying prone on the bottom, pretending to be lifeless, I tensed with the orca's approach. When he prodded my belly, I felt vulnerable; tension built as though I was going to explode. He nuzzled around, brushing my face with his chin. Becoming anxious when I didn't respond, he

Namu swimming upside-down with Ted on the whale's chin.

increased the probing and butting, rolling me over. Positioning himself directly overhead, Namu brought his door-sized flippers down with such force that I was lifted from the bottom in a torrent of swirling water. The orca swam under me, pressing his nose solidly to my belly. I couldn't move, pinned between the fast-moving whale and the pounding force of water pressure. By the time he had lifted me to the surface I was gasping for air.

Namu had treated me like the dolphins in folklore, which aided their injured companions, and occasionally rescued a sailor from the sea.

I pretended to sink, but Namu supported me by gently sculling his flippers, the rhythm of his undulating pulsing through my body. With arms outstretched, head tucked between, face pressed to his back, I felt a part of the whale. He was drawing me closer, holding, grasping my body, tugging at my mind.

A torrent of water pressed me ever tighter against his back. With my head awash, I was unable to breathe; the orca moved faster. I fanned my fingers; they caught the water, parting me from the whale, allowing a breath. Namu turned, pitching to one side like a ship; his sweeping tail cut a wide arc. I tingled in anticipation, waiting as the whale rose under me. He shifted for position, then started swimming at an even faster pace. I was enraptured. So often I had dreamed of moments like this, of me on his back, but now it was happening; this was real. The feeling was one of wild, uncontrollable joy. I wanted it to last forever.

Namu angled sharply upward. We breathed simultaneously. The whale seemed to perceive my more-frequent requirement for air.

I faced the orca, grasping his pectoral fins; we moved in unison like dancers, gliding through the water across our stage. At the slightest signal, my partner would turn this way or that. It was as though my every conscious wish became the whale's command. We twirled and twirled, and twirled again; then rose to breathe, and submerged once more.

My desire to be with the orca had become an addiction, no greater perhaps than his for me. In gaining acceptance from Namu, a highly intelligent and sensitive animal of immense capacity, I felt heightened awareness with all forms of life. Big problems seemed insignificant, little ones disappeared. Did I really understand the nature of this incredible creature? At every turn in our association I had asked, how well did I know the whale? The answer was another question, how well did I know myself?

"EEEE, URRH, EH."

"Yes, I hear you, but you say that about everything." Namu remained stationary in the center of the lagoon while I rested prone across his back. The whale, having nearly neutral buoyancy, had to inhale additional air to compensate for my added weight. Pressing my ear against him, I thought I heard the whale's heart beat; it was only mine. The tranquility and softness of my surroundings absorbed me; free of nagging restraint and interference, my mind soared. I was riding my orca in the open sea. Mariners passed in sailing craft and power boats, looking at us in disbelief. "A man," they shouted, "is riding a whale!" They would not report what they had witnessed. Who would believe them?

We journeyed until other orca came into view. They surrounded us amid squeals and splashing. I could hear them say, "It's true, a whale has befriended a man."

I awoke to sounds of waves lapping at the corkline, shifted my weight, and leaned on one elbow. Namu lurched; a tremble rippled through his body. "Did I startle you? You forget I was here?" He flexed his spine and lifted his pectoral fins, waking and stretching just like a horse would.

Much about him fitted my concept of the friend I would choose. His formal dress, tuxedo black and white, seemed to characterize him, always the perfect gentleman. His nature was to live, adapt when necessary, but survive. Understanding my shortcomings and limited swimming ability, he had accepted me, but only to the extent I had accepted myself. In a strange and unaccountable way, I loved the whale.

I reached my arms about Namu's dorsal, my cheek against his fin. Feeling the pressure of my knee on his flank, the whale turned for the dock, then whirled abruptly and swam toward deep water. I slipped off and swam the other way. The whale doubled back and caught me squarely, lifting me across his rostrum. "Hey, my friend, I'm cold, and hungry; we'll play again tomorrow." Crawling around behind the dorsal, I signaled for a ride to the float; he didn't obey. "And after all those nice things I said about you?"

I rolled from his back again, pushed off and stroked for shore. The huge white underbelly rose ominously from below. "Darn it, whale, enough is enough; I'm not built the same as you, though at times I wish I were. I must return to live on land." His pectoral flippers towered out of the water, over my head. The moment we touched, he clasped me gently but firmly in his "arms." A bewildering feeling overcame me, one of being loved by this wild yet sensitive behemoth. Though pressed to his chest, unable to break his grip, I was unafraid. Without releasing his hold, the whale rolled upright. His chest sagged as he exhaled, and then swelled with a new breath of air. When he turned upside down, I drew several quick breaths.

"Come on, Namu, how long are you going to play this game? Sure I wear a rubber suit which feels something like whale skin, and I've tried really hard to get you to like me, but, me your hostage? A whale keeping a man captive in a lagoon? Let me go!" I shifted a little, pushing on one huge flipper; it yielded. Slowly the whale's grip slackened; I slid from his chin into the water, still holding a flipper with one hand. The moment I let go, the whale lunged for me. "OK, OK." I quickly climbed on his back.

"Tom." The night watchman walked slowly out on the float. "Toss him a fish." The chunk of salmon landed a short distance away; Namu had it in seconds. "One more, Tom, alongside the float." When my friend dove for the food, I reached for the dock and pulled myself out of the water. Tom asked, "What was that all about?"

"Namu wasn't letting me out of the water."

"Maybe he thinks you are a whale and is worried about you."

"Yes, maybe so. After all, it's what I've always wanted."

Namu had fulfilled every wish I had hoped for when beginning my quest, to experience the life of a whale. Now I recognized those early visions and aspirations had been only a prelude to an even greater adventure. Between us there was a bond based upon respect, trust, and our desire to interact. I was obsessed with becoming that boy riding a dolphin, the one I had seen in a book as a child. The spirit of the whale inhabited me. Namu held me hostage for his pleasure as I had held him hostage for mine.

19
Parting of The Ways

Namu focused his attention fully upon me. Eager with anticipation, he quivered, ready to lunge on my slightest signal. Glistening in the sun, the indomitable, coal-black and snow-white creature radiated vitality. I shared with him this fine condition. "What a beautiful, lovable beast you are." Our lives had become so entwined, I scarcely remembered the time before we met.

As I had envisioned, the wild animal had become my closest companion, my teacher, and the source of a hundred new experiences. Others who met him had been enriched. Most discovered not only the whale, but an awakening within. If someone else's impossible dream had become reality, so might theirs.

Cruising the net, Namu eyed the open gate. "I understand, big fellow; you don't want to leave Rich Cove; neither do I. This is our home."

Here I had attained my fondest wish, but now I feared the loss of that enchantment. There seemed no alternative. The aquarium's star attraction had been sorely missed, the film company no longer paid his maintenance expense; and the cove's owners, frustrated with daily intrusions upon their privacy, had ordered that we leave. "Namu, are you hesitating because you know the new facility will be smaller? And the water, well, it's dirty. But you'll be there only a short while."

The word was out. "Namu has returned to Seattle." The excitement of the first show nearly immobilized me. I

197

put on my flashy, new red-and-blue dive suit. "Pete," I shouted, "give me a hand," my voice muffled inside the jacket.

"Put your arms over your head," Pete instructed as he yanked and tugged.

Walking to the ramp, I felt a little fire burning in my stomach. No show like this had ever been presented before. How would the whale react to a large audience surrounding him? What were they expecting? I wanted them to discover Namu as I had. The thrill for some would come when the matador confronted the bull; would the man survive the encounter? Others would see my interaction with the whale as entertaining, or as a process. A process in gaining understanding: of one's self, of the animal, and the nature of all life.

Where was the whale? At the feed station I continued to signal. Again no response. Hundreds of spectators peered into the dark water. "One moment, please," I said over the public address system. The sound of chuckles and laughter rippled through the anxious audience. Still no whale. Strapping on fifteen pounds of lead, I slipped into the water and descended through the murky surface-layer of Elliott Bay, searching for Namu in his one-hundred-foot-square enclosure. Halfway to the bottom, I found him in a school of black cod. The tasty fish didn't seem frightened, swimming in and out of the whale's open jaws; it was crunch and gulp, one after another. With a nodding head he greeted me, and I thought, *hope you're not too full of fish to perform.*

As we moved rapidly upward, the fish scattered before us. Breaking through the surface astride my "sea horse," I surprised the spectators who applauded and cheered as though the show had begun. I guess it had, though the intended order of events had been reversed. I stood on the whale's back as he cruised along the fence, then jumped away. Namu turned sharply, splashing the audience with a tail lob. He swam upside down, circling, waving his pectoral flippers. I climbed aboard and stood on his chin between the fins, tightly gripping the edge of one. He lowered me to the water, then lifted his fin, standing me up again.

With a salmon in hand, I swam toward the whale; he settled vertically, tail down. Grasping his chin with one hand, I dangled the fish overhead. Namu surged straight up, dragging me with him, higher and higher. Eight feet above water, hanging on with one arm, I peered through Namu's open jaws at astonished faces in the crowd. Dropping the food into his mouth, I let go, falling back with the whale.

The finale came when Namu leaped twenty feet to grab a suspended salmon. Though the audience had been warned, few stood back, and many were drenched in the whale's splash.

"Would anyone like to feed the killer whale?" A young woman stepped briskly to the platform, took the largest fish from the barrel, and leaned over the rail. She didn't jump back when the huge orca rose out of the water, letting him take the food from her hand. The smiling visitor even patted the nose as Namu fell back. Afterward I handed her a Polaroid snapshot recording the event. She was delighted, and back in the audience was surrounded by people. This proved so popular it became a regular part of the performance.

Frequently Namu saw me standing in the crowd between shows. He would swim over, turn upside down and open his mouth, trying to mooch a snack. I would hunch over and run along the walkway, but the whale wasn't fooled and followed.

Chatting with visitors, I never tired of telling them the story of how Namu and I came together, the fun of being with him, his training, my training. "Every day I try to do something new with the whale. Sometimes it is just the opposite—Namu does something new with me."

One day he had a towel in his mouth. He kind of waved it with a little head motion. I grabbed hold, trying to retrieve it. Sometimes animals swallow foreign objects which can block their stomach. Namu responded with a tug-a-war. He could not be tricked into releasing it. I ignored him; finally he let the towel go. I grabbed again, but the orca was too quick. He continued the new game, letting the towel drop, backing away, then pouncing when I tried to get it. I was mad, and swam after him. He just idled along, always staying exactly two feet ahead.

Next show he didn't have the towel. I worried about his stomach, but later he was waving his toy again. Several days afterward I found it on the bottom, abandoned.

Since the day I first found Namu eating the black cod that swam into his pen, I had offered him dead cod. It took a fair amount of effort to wean him, but once he decided to eat a variety of less expensive fish, the change was so swift I had to search for a buyer to take ten thousand pounds of frozen salmon off my hands.

The seventy-five foot water depth in Namu's sea pen allowed him to leap vertically, at times completely clear of the surface. Orca jump frequently in the wild, especially after leaving small bays and reaching open water. I have wondered what motivates them, joy, frustration, playfulness? Namu's spontaneous jumping eased my concern; perhaps he had adjusted to his new, more restrictive quarters.

"How are you coming with your plans for the new aquarium?" Homer asked, his voice heightened, anxious. "They going to let you build it?"

"The city council and mayor think it is a wonderful idea, but with all the adverse publicity from other sources I have laid low for a while. Certain people fear my competition if they are to get a tax-supported aquarium built. When the next site is found, I won't advertise my intensions. I'll just get a deal signed and proceed quietly."

"You may get a new site, but there are people who will make sure you never get a building permit. I wish it wasn't so. The whale shouldn't be left in Elliott Bay any longer than necessary."

"You mean the pollution?"

"Yes."

"If things don't work out soon, I'm going to put another liner under him and pump in filtered water. Right now I'm saving money for the new facility."

"That makes sense. Better allow more time for Namu. I think he misses your attention more than you realize."

"Thanks, Homer, I'll try to do that."

On the first hot day in June the sun was bearing down. I found the whale bobbing near the surface with just the tip of his snout showing. He had floated high in the water the previous day in the rain. I assumed he was protecting his sensitive skin from sunburn. A few days later he adopted the same profile minutes after the sun came out; the rest of the time he rested horizontal along the surface. It looked like he had learned something since last summer when he got a sunburn enroute to Seattle.

A small child about five or six stood with arms overhead, clutching the chain link fence, pressing his nose through the holes. Namu stirred. The boy pulled himself up a few inches and kicked his feet against the bottom rail. Namu turned toward the child. As the youngster let go and walked away from his parents, Namu swam over and followed him. Slowly the child realized the killer whale was tagging along. Reaching the next corner, the child ran back the way he had come, Namu at his side. The boy stopped, waved his arms at the orca, and ran the length of the dock. Namu, upside down, accompanied him. Around the corner they went, the little boy and his whale. Others began watching and pointing at the two. The mother finally scooped up her son as he swept by the third time. Namu stopped. I walked down the gangway, "That's OK, ma'am. Let your boy have fun. He's not hurting anything."

But the woman had seen enough. "No, thank you," she said; "I'll hang on to him. He's very active and might get a notion to climb the fence."

Yes, I thought, *I would have*.

There were more times like that, when Namu took a shine to someone and would follow. Often they did not recognize the whale's attention. When I pointed it out, they were frequently flabbergasted, "Why do you think he would follow me?"

"Perhaps your clothing caught his eye. Maybe it was the sound of your voice, or even what you were thinking."

"Thinking? That's incredible! A killer whale interested in people, even making choices about certain ones. Can he actually read my thoughts?"

"I think animals can 'read' other animal's thoughts and some people's as well. On occasions we humans get a telepathic glimpse of what another person is thinking; why not whales?"

At first I paid little attention to the occasional abrasions appearing on Namu's body, nor did I take notice of his slower responses. Then one day he swam under the walkway, carelessly swiping me off his back. I got a magnum headache from the blow. His dorsal suffered a bruise and sloughed several layers of skin. Though accepting a variety of fish, supplemented with vitamins and antibiotics, he became less and less interested in food. Namu's curiosity for new play objects diminished. "What's the matter with you, my friend? Bored? Not enough exercise?"

The whale's recent change in residence, his fourth in less than a year, was perhaps stressful, adding to his malaise. Though Elliott Bay would be free of raw sewage when the treatment plant was completed, the polluted water was highly objectionable to me, and surely was nearly intolerable for the orca. My plans for a new aquarium looked more distant than ever.

Almost a week passed; Namu was little changed. He ate about half his usual ration, but had to be coaxed. The trainers conducting some of the shows were able to get Namu to do most of his routine, but he gradually refused the food rewards.

"Ted, the call is for you."

"What's up?"

"You'd better come over right away. Namu's sick."

The sun was setting as I raced in Pegasus, from Bainbridge Island to Pier 56. I ran past a few late aquarium visitors leaning on the pier rail; their faces had a look of quizzical uncertainty. As I joined the staff huddled on the floats, someone said, "Namu's in a bad way. He took one fish with his vitamins and antibiotics this morning, but hasn't eaten since; been passing gas all afternoon and swimming erratically." My eyes were fixed on the whale.

He moved aimlessly near the center of his enclosure. His once sleek skin was checkered with cuts; many bled openly. The orca's bent-over dorsal was ragged and torn, like a flag after a storm. I felt a sudden urge to run, to escape—but there was no evading my own consciousness.

Namu's breathing became shallow, irregular, as was mine. "He's awful sick," one of the staff said quietly, "like he has the flu, and maybe a terrible pain."

"We'll have to restrain Namu; hold him up in the water. I'll go in and put a harness on him," I said.

"Ted, listen," Don tore his attention from the great whale that had become so much a part of our lives. His eyes were full of pain, but his jaw was set, muscles bulging, "There's no chance for that now. He's gone wild, out of his mind; he wouldn't know you. You'd be killed if you got in the pen."

Killed? The word jolted me. *It can't be true. Namu could never injure me.*

The eight-thousand-pound whale careened against the side of the float. "He's been bashing about like that for an hour."

"I've got to help Namu, Don. I must do something."

"Ted! Don't you understand? You can't help him. No one can."

"No! You're wrong. It's not too late. I **can** help him. I'll cut open the nets; let him go free. He'll be all right once he gets out of this dirty harbor." But deep inside I knew. I was conscious of a dry throat, pounding in my chest, and the gathering darkness. I felt feverish, weak. All thoughts blurred.

Namu's breach startled me. Turning to look, my neck vertebra snapped, sounding like the crack of lightning. The walkway gave a lurch as the animal smashed into the float again. I saw the look of horror on all the faces. The orca circled away, building speed, faster and faster. Again the mighty whale came, driving, thrusting his flukes, charging toward us in wild frenzy.

The walkway was awash, dragged under by the force of his impact with the steel nets. Time was slowing. My breathing slowed. I felt hollow, empty, alone. Beneath the gyrating float the whale struggled in a tangle of steel strands. I knew they were gripping his body, tighter and tighter, as the nets had once gripped mine in Warrior Cove. I had been trapped when they fell on me. *It's a mistake*, I had thought, *this can't be happening to me*. I sensed the pain as the wire strands cut through the whale's flesh. Rage was growing in me; fear, anger, helplessness.

Darkness had fallen. The shaking of the floats ceased. Time stopped. My world was strangely silent; I felt it had come to an end. Namu was dead.

Hisss-hushhh, hisss-hushh. Underwater, each reson-ant cycle of the regulator marked the passing of another moment in my existence. Suspended above was the sil-houette of the wild creature I had come to know—to know and to love. He had been the ultimate animal companion for me. I had sought an ideal, my desire to attain it so great that other values had become diminished or lost. I thought of my family and those who loved me, seeking strength and the will to live, but felt estranged. Time, and the whale, had come between us.

Shivering, unable to overcome the frightful cold that penetrated my body, I worked to free him from the tangle he had made in his death throes. My anger grew. All was black, nevertheless I saw him clearly, every inch of his body known to me. From under the shoulder, so often caressed, I gently removed strands of steel. A loose dock-piling's steady thump, thump, thump, cycling with each wave, sounded like the whale's heartbeat. A distant ray of light reflected in Namu's half-open eye startled me. For a moment I thought, perhaps . . . then burst into tears. It was the sudden, tragic death of my father all over again. I had felt I couldn't continue life without Dad. I had mourned his passing, attended his funeral and seen him buried, yet I could not accept the fact that he had died.

Continuing the work underwater, I thought, *Can't let them see you like this; must get you away, so you'll be remembered in all your former glory*. Tugging furiously on each tightly bound strand gained some slack to unloop it from around the whale. When finally Namu was free, the rage had subsided.

The line to Pegasus drew taut. I swam alongside my friend, helping, guiding him through the water, unable to comprehend that it was our last time together.

At Namu's autopsy a tooth was cut and the growth rings counted. He appeared to be seventeen years old, of a lifespan the scientists suggest can be thirty-five or more. His death was the result of an infection. The Seattle newspapers gave various accounts, one reporting the whale was lovesick and died by drowning in an attempt to be with his mate. When I pointed out the results of the autopsy, they refused to correct their fabricated, heart-rending story.

Namu had died from drowning, but the drowning was caused by *Clostridium perfringens*, an anaerobic bacteria which had grown and multiplied in the whale's digestive tract. The bacteria is usually present inside the whale, but the polluted water "insulted" the whale's system and enhanced the bacteria's growth. Namu was sick just a few days, primarily with a severe colic. Toxin affected his nervous system, causing the delirium which directly led to his death. Once identified, protection against the toxic bacteria could be provided. Later many orca were captured for public display and study. Most of them were innoculated with the toxoid, and none, to my knowledge, ever died from the disease which killed Namu.

20
Diplomats from Oceania

Parents told me their children were shocked to learn of Namu's unexpected death; they had cried and cried over the loss of their friend. I empathized with them, knowing how they suffered, and felt remorse for having encouraged others to identify with the whale. Some had loved him as I had.

I believed Namu could never be replaced, never equaled. At first I told myself he would come back, as I had believed my father would after he died. I had never faced the reality of death as a fact of life. It was a mystery which I had pushed away.

I talked with Joan about my grief. She said, "Ted, you must pull yourself together. You are disconnected from the real world. Namu's death was a loss to us all. Yours is greater of course, but life is a process: filled with change, starts and stops, new goals, new challenges. I know you think you can't replace Namu, and perhaps you are right. When Namu died, I watched some part of you die as well. That part will never flower again, but you will become stronger from the experience. I have never begrudged you that relationship. We all love you. Everyone wants to help; please let us."

Jim asked me to participate in several business ventures. I did, but with a minimum of interest. He would say, "When are you going to catch a replacement for Namu?" He spoke matter-of-factly, as though the cure for lovesickness was a new love.

"I'm trying, Jim. One of these days I'll do it." Though I

spoke with optimism about whales, and the future, I actually felt none of it would ever happen. My family were good listeners, but I didn't really allow them to help.

I wanted to see beyond my grief, to a time when I would feel good, when I could do work to my satisfaction. Now and then I lost a day somewhere, couldn't even remember it passing. I worked at small tasks, then gradually coped with larger ones.

I visualized killer whales, and tried to think what another one might be like. My imagination was blocked; I could get no sense of another whale's identity. All thoughts of starting over were bracketed in pain. I had loved Namu passionately, perhaps with the same capacity and energy that often exists between women and men. I had wanted to spend every minute with my companion. In the beginning there had been the desire to make friends, to overcome a killer whale's wild heritage. The book, *Island Stallion*, important in my childhood, had a boy hero who discovered a band of wild horses, then witnessed a battle to the death for supremacy. He felt drawn to the victor. It was that kind of challenge, the archetypal story, that had lingered in my subconscious.

I read in a magazine that Namu was alive and well, secretly hiding in Australia. So desperately did I long for his companionship that I found myself willing to believe the fictitious story. I wanted to shed my burden of guilt; I had brought Namu into the polluted water where the bacteria had killed him. My loved one died tragically, and indirectly by my own hand.

Slowly I found renewed strength. I was moving out of depression. It became reasonable to think there would be other whales and that I could feel something for them. Eventually it became possible to work towards such a goal, and after several whale-capture expeditions, Don and I succeeded. Nearly two years after Namu had died, we captured seventeen killer whales in Yukon Harbor near Seattle. I wondered how the orca would react to men in the water. Was Namu's lack of aggression unique? When the divers entered the eighty-by-eighty-foot holding pen to remove one animal, the corral was so crowded with killer whales that some divers had to push the huge sea mammals aside. Though highly stressed, and without food for a week, the wild orca were as gentle and friendly as Namu. We brought five back to the aquarium.

Sea World wanted several orca and sent their veterinarian to Seattle. Although his killer whale experience was limited to Shamu, his wide knowledge of sea mammals served us well. He cautioned, "You've got to get food into those animals right away."

"I'm trying to, Dave, but they refuse to eat."

"Do you have a food grinder?"

"No."

"Get one; and I'll show you how it's done."

As the water level dropped in the pool, five killer whales scooted on their bellies across the smooth floor, trying to join a favorite companion. Once stranded, each of the recently captured animals was covered with a wet bedsheet and watered continuously to prevent overheating. A rolled towel positioned behind each blowhole acted like a dam. It prevented hose water from running into the blowhole whenever opened for breathing.

"You'll have to get their mouths open," said the veterinarian. I pried on the jaws of the largest one, a fifteen footer, but couldn't budge them. "They're like horses, Ted; if you let them get the best of you now they'll be doubly difficult the next time." I coaxed and poked and pried. Nothing worked. Using my fingers to hike up the lips, I smeared a little fish stew against the teeth. The whale opened its jaws slightly; I inserted a broom handle. By working it back, I gained room enough for a two-by-four timber.

"Ah ha, got ya."

Pushing a wet, soft rubber hose into the killer's mouth, over the tongue and slowly, cautiously down the throat, I heard the veterinarian call out, "Be sure it's in the stomach, not the wind pipe."

"How can I tell?"

"The whale will let you know."

I started pumping in the concoction of ground fish, oil, vitamins, and food supplements. "Not too much the first day. Fifteen gallons is OK for that one." It took Don and me and our crew many hours of fussing around to get them all fed. We only had one bilge pump to work with.

Complete medical examinations were given the orca, together with innoculations against known cetacean diseases. Blood samples were taken for analysis.

When the valve was opened, water gushed into the pool. The two youngsters were the first to gain mobility, snuggling up to the larger whales, two females and a bull. Racing around like any kid underfoot, the five-hundred-pound babies knocked me over, cold water filling my chest-waders. The aquarium visitors watching the feeding had a good laugh, once they realized I was OK.

On the second day a remarkable change took place in the whales' attitude. Swinging their heads when I entered the pool, showing they recognized me, they tried to scoot over to the green pails of food. I gently stroked a lipline; the tongue emerged, tasting the formula. "That's it, big boy, you like this stuff. Mmmmmmmmmmn, goooood, come on, open up." With little difficulty I slid the four-foot rubber tube into the animal's stomach. The other whales talked, whistled, and called to one another while waiting their turn.

"Increase the amount today; twenty gallons for the large one, less for the others."

The two babies, between seven and eight feet long, were fed a formula similar to the adults, with a few additions. As their teeth hadn't erupted, I was resigned to continue the laborious tube-feeding process for several months. All the water would have to be let out of the pool three times a day. Although they were fun to play with, I didn't relish that commitment.

"Did you burp the babies, Ted?" my Seattle aquarium veterinarian asked.

"What do you mean, burp them?"

"Well, if you're going to mother those orca pups, you've got a lot to learn."

"Very funny, but I don't see you helping any," though I only jested, for Bill had attended the whales from the very first day of their capture.

"I'm the expert," Bill Klontz said. "Have to make sure you do it right."

Several days later I placed thousands of live herring in the pool. The smaller whales chased them like children after butterflies. Soon many fish were stunned and swam slowly. One baby took a straggler in its mouth, gumming it awhile, then swallowed the fish. Soon all five orca were in a free-for-all, chasing and gobbling the herring. At day's end they even scrounged dead ones from the bottom. I thawed some stored herring and tossed them into the pool. The whales ate them without hesitation.

"Looks like you'll make mother-of-the-month after all." The veterinarian could hardly suppress his smile.

Sea World purchased two of the five killer whales, and two were featured at my aquarium, Katy and Kandu. I was beseiged with requests for employment. They wrote, they phoned, they came to the aquarium and hung around. "And this one," Don said, "she's been here asking for a job every single day. She'll even work without pay if we let her be with the whales."

"I wish we had room for them all. Maybe we should start a training camp," I said.

The two of us strolled out to the pool. "Who is that in the water with Katy and Kandu?" I asked.

"Huh? oh, that's Jerry Watmore, one of the people I've been talking about." Dressed in a wet suit, the young woman swam between the two frolicking orca. Watching them took me back two years, to my time with Namu. Jerry appeared to have no fear as the whales thrashed around, bumping each other and her. She held the dorsal of each animal and they towed her between them around the pool. I admired her persistence in gaining access to the orca, and could see her natural inclination for working with them.

In the weeks that followed, Jerry's growing friendship with the whales seemed idyllic. I would have liked to see the three of them in the open sea. I wanted to offer advice, but restrained myself. She had the desire, patience, and endurance to attain her objective unassisted. I saw a happy future for her.

I felt left out, as though my time had passed. I yearned for another Namu, yet did not swim with the whales that were at the aquarium. During the recent capture, I was awestruck by the nearness of a magnificent bull and fantasied how I would befriend him, but was unable to see it through. I feared the emotional strain of making a new commitment. It appeared I would not allow the development of any deep, personal relationship, human or animal.

I took the fifth whale to Vancouver, B.C. for exhibition at Bob O'Loughlin's Boat and Sports Show. It had been nearly four years since we first talked of exhibiting a killer whale, and searched for one in Puget Sound. Though his Canadian show had been due to open in just a few weeks, Bob quickly arranged the necessary facilities.

Crossing the deserted Pacific National Exhibition grounds at dawn, I whistled to myself, unconsciously using my aquarium's wheee-uuuu-eee hustle-up call for trained animals. *Is someone else whistling?* I heard it again, then a spine-tingling shriek. I whistled once more; an answer came.

The night watchman had taken five minutes to let me in the previous day; now he was standing at the door asking quizzically, "How did he know you were coming?"

"Who?"

"Your friend here, Walter the whale. He's been making a terrible fuss."

"Killer whales are like that. They get lonesome."

Walter swam around his pool, head held high, peeking over the side. Water sloshed onto the floor as I leaped up the stairs. "Hi ya, fellow." He swam to me and pushed his chin over the edge. I dug in the ice chest and handed him several herring. "Gosh, whale, you're really something." Already we were becoming good friends. Only two weeks ago I had to stuff a two-by-four in his mouth to get the rubber feed-tube down.

When the doors opened, the visitors crowded around the whale and were unwilling to leave, preventing others a viewing opportunity. I devised a three-minute "whale show," mostly talking about Walter's recent capture, and handed out small fish to some spectators. "Thank you very much for coming today. Please exit down the stairway." The people moved on, handing their fish to Walter on the way. One visitor absent-mindedly carried the fish away with his exhibition literature.

Each hour two thousand more lined up to see the killer whale. I was surprised how quickly he picked up signals

and simple tricks, enjoying people. Floating near the pool-side, he allowed a dozen hands to rub him, then rolled upside down and offered his flipper, wanting to shake hands. The whale talked to his companions in Seattle, Katy and Kandu, via a telephone patch supplied by B.C. Telephone, and became a celebrity almost overnight. Vancouver residents treated the orca like royalty. Someone told me, "The only reason I came to this Boat Show was to see Sir Walter."

The Vancouver Public Aquarium showed great interest in the killer whale at the exhibition, but it wasn't until I was packing to leave that Gil Hewlett, the young biologist who had traveled with us on the Namu journey, arrived to say, "We'll take the whale at the price you quoted. It's all set. We have a truck on the way to pick him up."

Smiling, I said to Gil, "I'm really glad. The people here fell in love with that killer whale. I don't know how I could ever have taken Walter away from them. One thing, though, I can't guarantee the sex."

"That's OK; I understand. The mistake was made once before you know, with Moby Doll. This time we'll check before we name it."

So Walter was renamed Skana. Residing at first in a dolphin pool, then a new million-dollar killer whale exhibit, she broke all attendance records at the Vancouver aquarium, entertaining and educating viewers for thirteen years.

One incident from the Boat Show experience remains sharply focused in my memory. A man had watched intently as hundreds of hands touched the whale, then he turned to me, eyes filled with anguish. Slow in finding the right words, he began, "Are all killer whales like this one? sort of friendly?"

"I've met a lot over the years, and only once experienced an aggressive one. Namu was especially gentle,
even when I tried to anger him."

"But I've heard people tell how dangerous they are. I
always thought they would kill a man if given the chance."

"I know what you mean; I've heard such tales as well.
From their name it is easy to assume they are dangerous,
but to my knowledge no documented account of an orca
killing a person exists. The name stems from their practice
of killing other whales and sea mammals."

The visitor leaned on the pool wall, gripping the edge
until his knuckles turned white. "But aren't they something like sharks? You know what I mean?"

I nodded.

"They eat a lot of salmon, you know, cause trouble for
fishermen." I studied him as he talked. His hands were
broad and strong. I was convinced—given his manner and
appearance—that he was a fisherman. He said, "A while
back I came across some killer whales up north. They was
in a shallow bay; the tide had all but run out, squeaking
and whistling to one another, and . . ." He paused, drew a
breath, and with great effort, continued, "Just shot them
dead."

His words jolted me.

"Thought they were no good for nothing," he said,
struggling to maintain his composure, his eyes a little
murky. "I was thinking, what's a few blackfish, more or
less. When I was finished on them I didn't feel none too
good about it. One or two was still alive, I think. Now,
looking at this whale here, it's like seeing them again."

I felt like a priest listening to confession. The man
apparently had carried the burden for years. I replied, "At
times we all do things which we later cannot reconcile.
Others have spoken to me about shooting whales. They
had no purpose in doing so, but rather lacked a reason to

refrain. Once people become acquainted with these wild marine creatures the way you got to know this whale today, I am convinced that the senseless killing will end."

Clearly public attitudes were changing. For the most part killer whales were no longer ignored, nor feared, nor shot for sport. During Namu's autopsy a 303 Enfield rifle bullet was found lodged harmlessly in his blubber, indicative of the random pot-shots taken at orca in the past. Personalization of Namu and the public display of killer whales focused the attention of millions on these friendly intelligent mammals. New organizations were formed to capitalize on the changing attitudes. These groups raised money to attract public attention and exert political pressure for the purpose of saving the whales and other wild animals.

During our seven years together Don and I removed about thirty live killer whales from the wild. Several Canadian fishermen began capturing orca as well. Interest in killer whales became so great that we shipped them worldwide. Don or I personally escorted most of ours, with a guarantee of live delivery, to England, Japan, Australia, France, Germany, and throughout the United States. Millions of people became acquainted with these ambassadors from the kingdom of the sea: Namu, Shamu, Skana, Kandu, Kilroy, Ramu, Cuddles, Hugo, Ishmael, Ahab, Haida, and many others.

In time the organized groups and some individuals brought about the enactment of state and national legislation protecting marine mammals. Ironically this legislation put an end to the live capture of a few killer whales, but it did nothing to prevent other nations from annually harvesting many thousands of whales, including orca, for blubber.

From *Puget Soundings* magazine, May 1967

> Perhaps one of the greatest tributes to Ted's recent activities is, in fact, the criticism of those who bemoan the fate of the killer whale. Two years ago no one would have cared.

In response to a series of events with the whales, and the changing political climate, I retired from the aquarium and the whale business in 1972. Don continued. About a year before his retirement Homer gave me much of his photograph collection, covering his fifty years of capturing and training zoo animals. He left the aquarium in Seattle, settling in Portland, Oregon. Jim remains a businessman in Tacoma, Washington. Joan teaches school and raises the children on Bainbridge Island. I never did find another whale to take the place of Namu.

Many times my thoughts return to that incredible, lovable beast. I remember what the Eskimo in Namu, B.C. said to me. "Embodied within him is the spirit of man." Our association was only a beginning. Surely others will be allowed to follow, taking up the quest where I left off. Some individual will open a new door, unlocking further secrets, the only limit, their courage and imagination. They will interact with orca in the wild, and discover how to communicate with them. I look forward to that time.

ABOUT THE ILLUSTRATOR

Val Paul Taylor, his wife Karen, and two small children live in Mountlake Terrace, Washington just north of Seattle. He worked four and a half years as illustrator and book designer for Alaska Northwest Publishing Company, publisher of *Alaska* magazine and many books. With the commission for illustrating *Namu: Quest for the Killer Whale*, Val turned to free-lance work.

He attended art school in Ohio at Columbus College of Art and Design, then majored in Illustration and Graphic Design at Brigham Young University. He was born in Ogden, Utah. He has illustrated eight books and done the graphic design for several more. He won two awards for book graphic design, *Dale DeArmond, a first book Collection of her Prints* in 1980 and *A Guide to the Birds of Alaska* in 1981.

Val enjoys hiking, camping and Marx brothers' movies; coaches young people's basketball, and led a troop of Scouts to southeast Alaska in 1980 where they crossed the Chilkoot Pass out of Skagway.

Val says, "Illustration is a way of life for me. I love the challenge of different subjects. Whales fascinate me. I enjoyed expressing their beauty, intelligence, and vitality."

CAST OF CHARACTERS

Ted—Edward Irving Griffin   Jim—James Scott Griffin

Don—Donald G. Goldsberry   Homer Snow

Namu—*Orcinus orca*, Killer whale

The following people took part in the Namu story. In the interest of simplicity, some of them are not named in the text. The information applies until 1966.

Ch 1

Henry Willard Spaeth	stepfather
Nancy Mathewson Spaeth	mother
Edwin Lewis Griffin	father
Joan Holloway Griffin	wife
Cecil A. Brosseau	curator, Tacoma Municipal Aquarium

Ch 2

Duncan Bronson	suggested Ted build aquarium, insurance businessman
Randall H. Mull	carpenter in charge of aquarium construction
Paul Hansen	city building inspector, helped Ted get building permit
John Prescott	curator at Marineland of the Pacific
A.R. VanSant	pier owner, Seattle businessman
Gary Keffler	owner of Underwater Sports in Seattle, provided diver expertise, supplies, and personnel
Dale Dean	diver and raconteur

226

Ch 3
    Peter French   employed by Seattle Marine Aquarium

    Bob O'Loughlin   Portland, Oregon businessman and
                                   producer of sports and boat shows

    Lee Estes   gunsmith from Portland, Oregon

    Dr. Matthew Mayberry veterinarian associated with Portland Zoo

    Donald Potter   Seattle Police Department helicopter pilot

Ch 4
    Robert Rice   employed by Seattle Helicopter Airways,
                                   pilot of G–2 Bell helicopter

Ch 5
    Gary Boyker   public relations consultant for the Seattle
                                   Marine Aquarium

    Dell Rossberg   diver, rode six gill shark and Namu

Ch 6
    Lynn Campbell   owner and operator of Seattle Harbor
                                   Tours, adjacent to aquarium on Pier 56

Ch 7
    Dr. Murray Newman   director, Vancouver Public Aquarium

Ch 9
    Adam Ross   skipper of the purse seiner, Chinook,
                                   captured Shamu in 1965 and five orca in
                                   1967, resident Gig Harbor, WA

    Peter Babich   skipper of the purse seiner, Pacific Maid,
                                   participated in some whale captures,
                                   resident Gig Harbor, WA

    Don E. Vickery   employed by Lake Union Air Service, flew
                                   Ted on whale-scouting missions

Ch 10
    William Leckobit   three fishermen from Namu, B.C.,
    Robet McGarvey   joint-ventured to sell trapped whale
    Walter Piatocka

    Randy Sturtzer   body guard and escort for Ted

    Paul V. Thomas   free lance photographer on assignment for
                                   National Geographic

Ivar Haglund   Seattle restauranteur, Ivar's Acres of
                      Clams, Pier 54

Ch 11

Stephen Hunt   artist, fisherman, Bella Bella, B.C.

Vivian Wilson   skipper of fishing boat, Chamiss Bay,
                      towed pen to Port Hardy

Robert Hardwick   radio personality *extraordinaire*, Seattle

Bruce McKim   photographer for *Seattle Times*

Stan Patty   feature writer for *Seattle Times*

Gilbey Hewlett   biologist, Vancouver Public Aquarium

Emmett Watson   columnist for *Seattle P.I.*

George Losey   skipper, tug, Iver Foss, towed Namu's pen
                      to Seattle

Ch12

Robert d'Evers   owner of Canvas Supply Company, Seattle
McLauchlan   assembled lining for Namu's pen

Charles E. Peterson   owner of Trident Imports, occupied Pier 56
                      with aquarium

Ch 13

Theodore Walker,   scientist, Scripps Institute, La Jolla,
Ph.D.   California

James Fitzgerald   private contractor working for Office of
                      Naval Research, Anapolis, Maryland

Admiral Noel Gaylor   swam with Namu

Dr. Thomas C. Poulter Stanford Research Institute, Menlo Park,
                      CA, researched whale vocalizations

Dr. Merrill Spencer   Virginia Mason Research Center, Seattle,
                      investigated orca diving response

Ch14

Lamar Boren   cinematographer and underwater director
                      for the film, *Namu the Killer Whale*

Ivan Tors   producer of the film, *Namu the Killer Whale*

Ch16
Dr. David Kenney	veterinarian, Sea World
Gerald Brown	businessman, photographer, diver, member of whale-capture team, Everett, WA

Ch17
Jim Riddle John McLaughin	two divers working on the Namu film
William E. Garrett	Illustrations editor for *National Geographic*
Flip Schulke	freelance photographer specializing in underwater work, Miami, Florida
Laslo Benedek	director for film, *Namu the Killer Whale*
Robin Mattson Lee Meriwether Bob Lansing	three stars of the Namu film
James Halpin	journalist for *Seattle* magazine

Ch18
Tom Harper	caretaker for Namu while at Rich Cove

Ch20
Dr. G. William Klontz	veterinarian and mammalogist for the Seattle Marine Aquarium
Jerry Watmore	employed by Seattle Marine Aquarium trained killer whales

---

Jay Edward Griffin Jon Frederic Griffin Gaye Elizabeth Griffin Jill Parks Griffin	Ted's children live on Bainbridge Island with their mother. They didn't get to know Namu. At that time Jay was three, Jon was two, and Gay was eight months, born during the capture of Shamu. Jill was born three years later.

COLOPHON

Typeface	Palatino set 12 on 14
Typesetting	by computer, Mergenthaler 202N Nova Typesetting, P.O. Box 6215 Bellevue, WA 98007
Printing	lithography, sheet fed, offset press Publishers Press, 1900 West 2300 South Salt Lake City, Utah 84119
Binding	smyth sewn, hardbound, kivar #5
Paper	smooth white, 70 pound, offset
Illustrations	halftones on 133 line screen
Photographs	a, Ektachrome, Gary Keffler b, c, Kodachromes, Merrill Spencer paper, 80 pound gloss
Dust Jacket	cover photograph ⊙National Geographic, Flip Schulke, Black Star cover photo color-enhanced, Al Doggett author's portrait, Wallace Ackerman graphic design, Val Paul Taylor
Editorial Consultants	Barbara Noland O'Steen Charles Schuster, University of Washington

INDEX